Oxford Shakespeare Topics

Shakespeare and Work

OXFORD SHAKESPEARE TOPICS

Published and Forthcoming Titles Include:

David Bevington, *Shakespeare and Biography*
Colin Burrow, *Shakespeare and Classical Antiquity*
Michael Caines, *Shakespeare and the Eighteenth Century*
Lawrence Danson, *Shakespeare's Dramatic Genres*
Mario DiGangi, *Shakespeare and Queer Studies*
Janette Dillon, *Shakespeare and the Staging of English History*
Paul Edmondson and Stanley Wells, *Shakespeare's Sonnets*
Gabriel Egan, *Shakespeare and Marx*
Sonya Freeman Loftis, *Shakespeare and Disability Studies*
David Fuller, *Shakespeare and the Romantics*
John S. Garrison, *Shakespeare and the Afterlife*
Andrew Gurr and Mariko Ichikawa, *Staging in Shakespeare's Theatres*
Jonathan Gil Harris, *Shakespeare and Literary Theory*
Russell Jackson, *Shakespeare and the English-speaking Cinema*
Alexa Alice Joubin, *Shakespeare and East Asia*
John Jowett, *Shakespeare and Text: Revised Edition*
Douglas Lanier, *Shakespeare and Modern Popular Culture*
Hester Lees-Jeffries, *Shakespeare and Memory*
Ania Loomba, *Shakespeare, Race, and Colonialism*
Raphael Lyne, *Shakespeare's Late Work*
Russ McDonald, *Shakespeare and the Arts of Language*
Randall Martin, *Shakespeare and Ecology*
Steven Marx, *Shakespeare and the Bible*
Robert S. Miola, *Shakespeare's Reading*
Marianne Novy, *Shakespeare and Outsiders*
Lois Potter, *Shakespeare and the Actor*
Phyllis Rackin, *Shakespeare and Women*
Catherine Richardson, *Shakespeare and Material Culture*
Tom Rutter, *Shakespeare and Science*
Duncan Salkeld, *Shakespeare and London*
Will Sharpe, *Shakespeare and Collaborative Writing*
Stuart Sillars, *Shakespeare and the Victorians*
Bruce R. Smith, *Shakespeare and Masculinity*
Zdeněk Stříbrný, *Shakespeare and Eastern Europe*
Michael Taylor, *Shakespeare Criticism in the Twentieth Century*
Alden T. Vaughan and Virginia Mason Vaughan, *Shakespeare in America*
Gary Watt, *Shakespeare and the Law*
Stanley Wells, ed., *Shakespeare in the Theatre: An Anthology of Criticism*
Martin Wiggins, *Shakespeare and the Drama of his Time*

Oxford Shakespeare Topics

FOUNDING EDITOR: STANLEY WELLS

GENERAL EDITORS: LENA COWEN ORLIN AND PETER HOLLAND

Shakespeare and Work

MICHELLE M. DOWD

OXFORD
UNIVERSITY PRESS

OXFORD
UNIVERSITY PRESS

Great Clarendon Street, Oxford, OX2 6DP,
United Kingdom

Oxford University Press is a department of the University of Oxford.
It furthers the University's objective of excellence in research, scholarship,
and education by publishing worldwide. Oxford is a registered trade mark of
Oxford University Press in the UK and in certain other countries.

Published in the United States of America by Oxford University Press
198 Madison Avenue, New York, NY 10016, United States of America

British Library Cataloguing in Publication Data
Data available

Library of Congress Control Number: 2026941578

ISBN 9780198896074 (hbk)
ISBN 9780198896098 (pbk)

DOI: 10.1093/9780191998096.001.0001

Printed and bound by
CPI Group (UK) Ltd., Croydon, CR0 4YY

MIX
Paper | Supporting
responsible forestry
FSC® C013604
FSC
www.fsc.org

The manufacturer's authorized representative in the EU for product safety is
Oxford University Press España S.A. of Parque Empresarial San Fernando de Henares,
Avenida de Castilla, 2 – 28830 Madrid (www.oup.es/en or product.safety@oup.com).
OUP España S.A. also acts as importer into Spain of products made by the manufacturer.

Acknowledgments

I would like to thank Ellie Collins at Oxford University Press for her belief in this project and her encouragement during the many years that I've been working on it. I'm especially grateful for her guidance as I reimagined this book for the Oxford Shakespeare Topics Series, a process begun during the Covid-19 pandemic. My thanks go as well to the Series Editors, Stanley Wells, Peter Holland, and Lena Cowen Orlin, for their support, and to the Press's anonymous reader for helpful suggestions beginning at the proposal stage. I'd also like to thank Rachel Atkins at Oxford University Press for her assistance as I prepared the manuscript, Ponneelan Moorthy and all others involved in the production process, and Susan Certo for preparing the index.

I shared ideas from this book at various professional settings over the past decade or so, and I am grateful for the many interlocutors that helped me frame (and reframe) individual chapters and arguments. Particular thanks go to Kim Coles and Amanda Bailey for hosting me as part of the Marshall Grossman Lecture Series at the University of Maryland in 2016, Scott Newstok and Stephanie Elsky for welcoming me to Rhodes College for the Pearce Shakespeare Lecture in 2019, and Ari Friedlander for inviting me to speak on this topic for the James Edwin Savage Lecture in the Renaissance at the University of Mississippi in the fall of 2025. I also benefited from the conversations I had with participants and audience members during several seminars and panels at the Shakespeare Association of America and the Renaissance Society of America annual conferences. For their feedback at these conferences, I would especially like to thank Hillary Eklund, Jean Feerick, Laura Kolb, Jonathan Lamb, Jeremy Lopez, Paula McQuade, Dorothy Todd, and Rob Wakeman. I am grateful as well to Tom Rutter for inviting me to participate in a seminar on "Everyday Shakespeare" at the World Shakespeare Congress in Stratford-upon-Avon in 2016; in addition to Tom, my thanks go to Katherine Attié, Nandini Das, and the other seminar participants for their thoughtful comments and feedback. Many other scholars shared their insights and offered advice at various stages of the writing and research process. In particular, I would like to thank Risa Applegarth, Lara Dodds, Jen Feather, Jean Howard, Jennifer Keith, Natasha Korda, Penelope Geng, and Amy Vines.

The general outlines for this book began to take shape just before I joined the faculty at the University of Alabama in 2016. Since that time, I've had the great fortune to work with an amazing group of colleagues who have sustained my work throughout its many stages. Department Chairs Joel Brouwer, David Deutsch, and Steven Trout provided invaluable support during the years that I was working on this book. I am especially grateful for a research sabbatical in the fall of 2021, which gave me the time and resources to reimagine this project for the Oxford Shakespeare Topics series. My fantastic colleagues in the Hudson Strode Program in Renaissance Studies, including David Ainsworth, Alex Cook, Tricia McElroy, Cassie Smith, and Elizabeth Tavares, are an ongoing source of encouragement and intellectual camaraderie. The University of Alabama is also home to a wonderful community of early modernists beyond the English department, and I have benefited enormously from their intellectual generosity and spirit of exchange. My thanks in particular go to Fabio Battista, Jessica Goethals, Tanja Jones, Lucy Kaufman, and Daniel Riches. During my time at the University of Alabama, I've also had the privilege to work with an amazing group of students, especially graduate students in the Hudson Strode Program in Shakespeare Studies. I am truly grateful to all of them, and I count myself lucky every day to have the opportunity to work with such a talented and brilliant group of early modernists.

Finally, my deepest thanks go to my parents, Frank and Pat Dowd, who continue to be an unwavering source of love and support, and to my wonderful husband, Mike Cowie, for sharing this journey with me.

Contents

List of Illustrations

Note on Texts

Unless otherwise indicated, all quotations from Shakespeare are taken from *William Shakespeare: The Complete Works*, ed. Stanley Wells and Gary Taylor, 2nd edition (Oxford: Clarendon Press, 2005). When quoting from early modern editions, I have modernized spelling and punctuation for ease of reading.

Introduction: Shakespeare, Work, and the Everyday

What does it mean to work? As readers in the twenty-first century, we might initially respond to this question with a general list of synonyms: Toil. Labour. Exertion. Drudgery. Job. Career. Grind. Chore. Task. Industry. Effort. Endeavour. But a basic list of words cannot fully convey the complexity and variety of work, the specific and wide-ranging occupations and daily tasks that fill most of our lives and that have significance beyond the tasks themselves. Work shapes our identities, it can affect where we live and how we organize our days, and it influences how we relate to those around us. Indeed, how, when, and where we work, and how we are compensated (or not) for our labour has an impact on nearly every aspect of our lives. Work is not just something that we *do.* It is something that changes who we are and how we engage every day with the world in which we live.

The same was true in Shakespeare's day. But what did work mean to Shakespeare? And what does it mean to work in Shakespeare's plays? We might start to answer these questions by turning our attention to some of his most famous working characters: Bottom the weaver and his fellow artisans—Quince, Flute, Snout, Snug, and Starveling—who so memorably entertain the onstage and offstage audiences in *A Midsummer Night's Dream*. Identified by their specific occupations in the text (carpenter, weaver, bellows-mender, tinker, joiner, and tailor), Bottom and his coworkers are described as '[h]ard-handed men that work in Athens here' (5.1.72) and as 'rude mechanicals' who 'work for bread upon Athenian stalls' (3.2.9–10). They are thus clearly associated with physical labour—work that earns them bread and literally hardens their hands—and identified as workers in the comic world of the play. But we never actually see them doing any of this work onstage: Bottom never weaves and Starveling, the tailor, never mends clothes. What they do instead is rehearse and stage a laughably bad play. But is that work? And why might Shakespeare have singled out these characters according to their occupations and then connected them to theatre in this way? Work is clearly an important thematic focus for Shakespeare in *A Midsummer Night's Dream*, one he uses to create some of his most richly drawn comic characters. But what exactly does it mean to stage work in Shakespeare's theatre?

We will return to the mechanicals in *A Midsummer Night's Dream* when we explore artisans and apprentices in Chapter 4. But even this brief glimpse at a few of Shakespeare's most notable working characters raises important questions about the relationship between theatre and work that we will consider throughout this book. In many ways, *Midsummer* is a fairly obvious place to start thinking about work in Shakespeare, since it features artisan workers as central, memorable characters. But this comedy also opens up more complex questions about *how* work gets represented onstage and how incorporating work—whether through the inclusion of working characters, scenes of actual onstage labour, or verbal allusions to work—affects the dramatic narrative Shakespeare is telling. What we see specifically in *A Midsummer Night's Dream* is that work is not only central to the comedic subplot, but it is also closely linked to theatre and performance. Bottom and his coworkers are meant to be taken lightly, even laughed at. But they are also earnest, well-meaning artisans who ultimately steal the show and win the affection of at least the offstage audience (and generations of readers). The play thus connects the working world of Bottom and his compatriots to the working world of the theatre more broadly. In making these connections, *Midsummer* draws attention to some of the practical realities of theatrical culture in Shakespeare's England. As we will explore in more detail in the next two chapters, the early modern theatre was deeply indebted to the London craft guilds, which dated back to the medieval period. Shakespeare's theatre, therefore, was not simply a place where ideas about work could be staged; it was a workplace in its own right. As a result, work is far from a simple category for Shakespeare: it is instead an animating feature of much of his drama, one that influences in often subtle and surprising ways the central dramatic questions—about theatre, about identity, about human relationships, about society, about justice—that Shakespeare returns to repeatedly throughout his career. This book argues that we can come to a richer understanding of Shakespeare's dramatic output if we attend to how the everyday world of work shapes the fabric of his plays.

Work is such a basic part of our own contemporary lives that we might sometimes take it for granted or not think it deserves much critical attention. And yet, we can easily see how work shapes virtually every aspect of our lives. It structures our time (our daily schedules, the work week, retirement age); it defines our space (office configurations, work-from-home arrangements, the daily commute); it shapes our familial and social relationships (the idea of one's career or career-track, status, working roles within the family); and it even influences how we think about *not* working (leisure time, weekends, post-work retirement, work–life balance). Certainly, the circumstances of twenty-first-century working life differ significantly from those of Shakespeare's England in the sixteenth and seventeenth centuries, but work was nevertheless as crucial a part of early modern society as it is for us today. And just as today we are witnessing significant shifts in our working lives (through changes in technology and the increased emphasis on developing work–life balance, for instance), the early modern period saw its own series of cultural and economic shifts that affected how work was understood. The fact that work is a pervasive component of both early modern and contemporary life, then, does not mean that it is insignificant or undeserving of commentary—quite the contrary. And the more carefully we look at Shakespeare's plays, the more we see just how important work, and the numerous ideas and debates that surround that work, are to his dramatic worlds.

The world of work—including the men and women at all social levels who performed it—was vital to Shakespeare's drama, both because the theatre was a highly successful business enterprise and because work significantly influences the plot, language, and structure of Shakespeare's plays throughout his career. This book will introduce readers to the rich working world of Shakespeare's plays. To do so, it will take up questions such as: where do we see work *at work* in Shakespeare? How do we know where to look for it, especially when certain forms of work (such as agricultural labour or the everyday labour of artisans, as we saw in *Midsummer*) are rarely if ever staged directly? What dramatic and poetic tools does Shakespeare turn to in order to represent work in his plays? And what does attending to work in Shakespeare teach us about his artistry as well as about his impact on contemporary readers and students today? This book focuses on how Shakespeare's dramatic oeuvre engages in vital ways with the early modern world of work, and it argues that a better understanding of that engagement can help inform our interpretation of Shakespeare's dramaturgy and our assessment of his cultural legacy.

Defining Work in Shakespeare

Work may be a quintessential part of both early modern and contemporary life, but it is a remarkably difficult concept to define precisely. If we define work as exertion, for instance, then it becomes a broad enough category to include strenuous leisure activities, such as playing sports or dancing. But if we define it as paid labour, then we are excluding enforced work, such as enslaved labour. Perhaps we could identify certain activities that count as work? Here, too, we run into challenges. If I go out on the weekend and dig in my garden, is that work? Or is it only work if I'm formally employed as a gardener? The same activity may be viewed quite differently, depending on the social context in which it is taken. The difference between work and non-work, as sociologists and historians have pointed out, usually can't be located by pointing to something inherent in the activity itself. Instead, an activity counts as work based on the context in which it is performed.[1] Work is thus not a stable or fixed category, but one that is malleable and open to debate, based on changes in social circumstances or cultural values.

The fact that work can be such a fluid category makes it a particularly rich topic for Shakespeare to explore in his plays. Work is fundamentally a *relational* category: its meaning and significance is never intrinsic, but instead changes based on one's perspective or immediate framework, as the example of gardening suggests. As a result, any discussion of work—especially work in the distant past—requires that we think carefully about context: who is performing it, when, where, and under what circumstances? In Shakespeare's England, the word 'work' could certainly refer to a wide range of practices, ranging from the generic ('a thing to be done') to the surprisingly specific ('the process of making a textile fabric').[2] Furthermore, work was often defined in explicit opposition to something else, something that was considered *not* work. Even today we often think about work in terms of what it *isn't*: play isn't work, rest isn't work, and leisure time isn't work time. Writers in Shakespeare's England often turned to binary oppositions to define work. As Tom Rutter notes, in early modern England, '[a]cting is considered by some commentators to be work, but others not; gentlemen and nobles are represented as workers who serve the realm through non-manual labour, but the idea that to be a gentleman is to be idle remains widespread'.[3] The concept of work in Shakespeare's England was thus very much open to debate.

Indeed, ideas about the fundamental nature of work and who should perform it were changing in early modern England, so much so that 'definitions of work became hot issues' in the period.[4] Broadly speaking, there was a shift from a pre-Reformation idea of work as a 'painful duty carried out by those who laboured with their hands' to an understanding by the sixteenth century that work was 'an obligation incumbent upon all'.[5] Idleness and inactivity were to be avoided at all costs, while the *vita activa* (the active life) came to be seen as a moral good as well as a social and economic necessity. These changes, which we will survey in more detail in Chapter 1, meant that work was an especially urgent topic in early modern England, one that was directly related to almost every aspect of early modern life. Shakespeare's theatre provided an ideal space in which to explore the changing nature of work and its broader significance because, by the very nature of the dramatic conflicts it staged, the theatre emphasized a multiplicity of perspectives rather than a single vision or interpretation. Shakespeare's diverse range of characters, plots, and images, in other words, bring the early modern world of work to life with all its messiness, complications, and vitality.

Not surprisingly, then, scholars have often turned to Shakespeare's plays to examine how he stages various forms of labour. As early as the 1920s, for instance, Charles W. Camp wrote about Shakespeare's representations of craftspeople and apprentices in *The Artisan in Elizabethan Literature*. Although Camp asserted that Shakespeare's views of working people were largely negative, other commentators came to very different conclusions. In *Shakespeare the Craftsman*, for example, M. C. Bradbrook argued that Shakespeare's creative artistry was inseparable from his own understanding of theatre as a craft.[6] Scholars in more recent years have tended to follow Bradbrook, taking a more nuanced view of the playwright's engagement with work and working people. Those working in Shakespeare studies have also expanded the discussion of labour to include not only craftspeople, but also servants, enslaved people, domestic workers, actors, merchants, and agricultural workers, to name just a few.

Contemporary approaches to Shakespeare and work draw heavily on what has come to be known as 'materialist criticism'. In general terms, this approach considers literary texts in relation to the economic, social, and historical conditions of their creation. Materialist criticism is not equivalent to Marxist criticism, but the two approaches share some important perspectives, including the basic interest in connecting literary texts to the specific economic circumstances under which they were produced.[7] As Gabriel Egan has noted, 'For students of literature Marx's most important work is on the relationship between creativity and economic production.'[8] Similarly, materialist critics are interested in how literary texts engage with the socio-economic world in which they were created, a process that is always dynamic and multidimensional. Literary texts, in other words, do not simply 'reflect' historical realities; they also help to shape how readers and audiences perceive and respond to the world around them. By the same token, the culture in which a given literary text (such as a Shakespeare play) was written and performed is not a static 'background', but instead a complex and varied landscape. Practically speaking, most materialist Shakespeare critics tend to take a broad view of the various 'material' features that can shape a given play or poem. These approaches thus situate the literary text as part of a wider, cultural frame of reference that includes things like social status, gender, familial relationships, race, marital status, and occupational identity. Since work was such a central feature of everyday life in early modern England, as it is today, it is no surprise that discussions of Shakespeare and work have tended to take materialist critical approaches.

As a result of its indebtedness to materialist criticism, scholars interested in work in Shakespeare have tended to privilege staged rather than described instances of labour, focusing primarily on characters explicitly identified as workers or scenes in which we see characters performing work onstage. So, for example, scholars have drawn attention to the mechanicals in *Midsummer* or have analysed selected scenes in which characters perform manual labour (such as when Ferdinand is forced to carry logs onstage by Prospero in *The Tempest* in order to prove himself a worthy suitor of Miranda) or enact administrative or domestic duties (such as when Feste and Maria in *Twelfth Night* manage the business of Olivia's household). The result is that more attention has been given to concrete and readily recognizable forms of labour than to types of work that are marginal, informal, or simply alluded to in the plays. This critical tendency is, of course, quite understandable since work is an embodied act that is almost always demonstrated through some kind of direct action in the world. Additionally, as we have seen, the nature of work itself is often amorphous and difficult to define. By concentrating on more tangible forms of labour, critics in the field help ensure that our discussions about work in Shakespeare remain similarly specific in focus. However, such approaches also run the risk of codifying certain activities (weaving, acting, service) as work while neglecting others that might seem more ephemeral or more challenging to represent on the early modern stage (certain kinds of domestic work, farming, overseas commerce). Instead of devoting our attention exclusively to the small handful of Shakespeare's plays that have received the most analysis in terms of work—plays like *Midsummer*, *2 Henry VI*, and *The Tempest*—this book argues that we can gain deeper insights by broadening our perspective, by moving beyond the usual suspects and considering how Shakespeare represents various types of work throughout his dramatic career—including in plays not usually thought about in terms of work.

Methods and Approaches

In order to expand our understanding of Shakespeare's treatment of work in his plays, this book draws on a range of critical approaches. Materialist analysis is certainly a central feature of the chapters that follow, and we will look carefully at how Shakespeare stages work and working people, including in the plays mentioned above as 'usual suspects'. Reading characters like Bottom and his coworkers in *Midsummer* or Caliban in *The Tempest* by locating them with the complex socio-economic world in which they were created helps open up a richer awareness of these figures and the plays in which they appear. We will consider in Chapter 4, for instance, how Shakespeare's depiction of the mechanicals was influenced by contemporary events, such as the 1596 uprising of artisans and apprentices, and we will discuss in

Chapter 3 how his staging of Caliban reflects and comments upon emerging understandings of race in the context of the transatlantic slave trade. All chapters take the complex and sometimes contradictory nature of both the literary text and the broader world in which it was created as a given: text and context are never entirely separate from each other, and neither is ever inert or merely a reflection of the other. As a result, the materialist focus of this book will be deliberately broad in scope, incorporating the study of gender and sexuality, race, and class, among other critical perspectives, in order to help us more fully examine Shakespeare's depictions of work in his plays.

But in addition to its materialist focus, this book will also explore how Shakespeare's dramatic *language* is often inspired by the everyday world of work. If we concentrate exclusively on work that is staged, we risk losing sight of the important role of aesthetic features, such as metaphor and rhetorical language, in Shakespeare's drama. As Russ McDonald writes, 'Shakespeare's language functions as a symbolic register, an instrument for recording, transmitting, and magnifying the conditions of the fictional world that the play represents—the conflicts, affinities, and changes occurring among the persons who inhabit it.'[9] Figurative language can amplify and even alter what we see on stage, but it can also conjure up images and ideas that are never directly staged at all. So, even in plays where no discernible work is performed by characters onstage, we can find poetic imagery drawn from the world of work, including references to harvests, allusions to shopkeepers, and colloquial language associated with apprentices. By exploring not only plays explicitly about labour or individual scenes of labour or characters who labour, but also how Shakespeare's texts deploy the language of labour, this book integrates materialist and aesthetic approaches to show just how extensively ideas and debates about work animate Shakespeare's plays.[10]

A quick comparison between Shakespeare and other early modern playwrights may be instructive here. Some of Shakespeare's contemporaries wrote in a dramatic genre known as city comedy. These plays were set predominantly in London or other urban settings and typically focused on issues related to social class, commerce, and trade. Playwrights such as Thomas Dekker, Ben Jonson, and Thomas Middleton were especially well known for writing in this genre, which often depicted everyday economic situations onstage, such as apprentices at work in a shop or women selling commercial goods in the street. Dekker's 1599 comedy *The Shoemaker's Holiday*, for instance, tells the story of Simon Eyre, a master shoemaker who later becomes sheriff and Lord Mayor of London. Numerous scenes in the play feature Eyre in his shop with his apprentices and journeymen making shoes and conducting business with customers. Shakespeare, however, was not known as a writer of city comedy (the closest he came to city comedy was, arguably, in *Measure for Measure* and to a lesser degree in *The Merry Wives of Windsor*).[11] Compared with contemporary examples such as *Shoemaker*, then, Shakespeare's approach to labour in his plays looks a bit different.

Of course, Shakespeare, as we've seen, does put workers and their labour directly onstage, in plays such as *The Tempest* and *Midsummer*. In *The Tempest*, for instance, both Caliban and Ferdinand carry logs and firewood onstage. In Act 2, scene 2 Caliban enters 'with a burden of wood', and in the next scene, Ferdinand enters the stage 'bearing a log' (3.1; Figure 1.1). But these two forms of labour, which may look indistinguishable from each other onstage, differ in very important ways. Ferdinand's labour, which is imposed upon him by Prospero to make his 'winning' of Miranda more difficult so that he values that 'prize' more highly (1.2.454–5), is temporary and presented as part of the play's romantic plotline that ultimately brings Ferdinand and Miranda together. Ferdinand tells us that he 'must remove | Some thousands of these logs and pile them up', but he assures the audience that because he performs this work to win Miranda's love and Prospero's approval, his 'labours' become 'pleasures' (3.1.9–10, 7). Physical work in this scene functions as an embodied metaphor for heterosexual romantic courtship: Ferdinand's labour translates his efforts to win Miranda's love into a concrete and highly visible form onstage.

Caliban's similar onstage labours take on quite different meanings. Unlike Ferdinand, he is identified with enforced manual labour before he even appears onstage. Prospero calls for Caliban, his 'slave', whom he describes to Miranda as one who 'does make our fire | Fetch in our wood, and serves in offices | That profit us' (1.2.310, 313–15). His work is not temporary, but a permanent condition directly associated with his bondage to Prospero. We will discuss Caliban in the context of service and slavery again in Chapter 3, but for now we can note that

Figure 1.1 Ferdinand carrying logs in *The Tempest* (3.1). Drawing by Johann Heinrich Ramberg (1830). Courtesy of the Folger Shakespeare Library.

Shakespeare deliberately draws the audience's attention to seemingly identical acts of labour (carrying wood) and invites us to consider how and why they resonate so differently onstage. These acts of labour, like the example of gardening mentioned earlier, mean very different things because of the context in which that labour is performed. When Shakespeare stages work directly, as he does in *The Tempest*, he often does so to highlight the relational nature of work and raise vital questions about status, freedom, and identity.

We will discuss scenes such as these throughout this book, as they can help us understand how work often shapes Shakespeare's plots and his development of character. But onstage scenes of work are only one part of the picture. Indeed, Shakespeare's plays more often represent labour through imagery, allusions, or language related to specific occupations rather than through staged action. In these instances, work is not entirely absent from the stage, but is instead present indirectly in an exchange of dialogue, a provocative phrase, or even an individual word. In part, this reliance on figurative language is the result of Shakespeare's preferences for specific dramatic genres: his penchant for English and Roman history plays, tragedies, and romantic comedies means that there is little occasion in his oeuvre for the kinds of scenes of everyday work found in city comedies such as *The Shoemaker's Holiday*. But the connection between labour and Shakespeare's dramatic language is also a result of the working conditions of the theatre itself (which we will explore more fully in Chapters 1 and 2). Put simply, there were certain limitations to what could be staged in the early modern theatre. Without recourse to elaborate sets to establish locale, for instance, Shakespeare's theatre relied instead on the use of small props and costumes, verbal references to offstage actions, and dramatic imagery that conjured up a vivid and complex world for the audience. Alan Dessen refers to this process as a kind of 'theatrical shorthand' or 'theatrical synecdoche', in which 'Shakespeare asks his audience to accept a part for the whole, to supply imaginatively what cannot be introduced physically onto the open stage'.[12] We can see this kind of imaginative invitation at work in the famous choric Prologue than opens *Henry V*. The Chorus apologizes for the limitations of the stage ('this unworthy scaffold'), which cannot sufficiently represent the 'vasty fields of France' or the full-scale battle of Agincourt. Instead, the Chorus asks the audience to take an active role in the dramatic entertainment by 'piec[ing] out our imperfections with your thoughts'. In other words, the audience should 'Think, when we talk of horses, that you see them', because ''tis your thoughts that now must deck our kings' (Pro. 10, 12, 23, 26, 28). The Chorus is discussing the ability of the early modern stage to depict warfare, but this speech is just as relevant to our understanding of how the stage was able to represent work. Throughout his career, Shakespeare routinely invites his audience to 'piece out our imperfections with your thoughts', supplying the creative analysis to fill in the blanks of what is not (or cannot be) staged. In this sense, the audience is a vital collaborator in bringing these plays to life, if we take the lead that Shakespeare's language gives us.

So, while directly staging the entire panoply of the early modern working world was beyond the limits of the early modern platform stage, Shakespeare could draw on that world through metaphor, simile, and allusive references, as well as through the strategic use of props and costumes. As Caroline Spurgeon notes in *Shakespeare's Imagery and What It Tells Us*, Shakespeare demonstrates 'a knowledge of numbers of trades or crafts and their processes, and draws upon many of them repeatedly for his similes'.[13] Shakespeare's plays thus challenge us to 'read' work differently by encouraging us to pay attention to how work enters the theatre both directly, through the physical details of staged scenes, and indirectly, through elements of the dramatic text such as imagery and speech patterns. Such references do not typically provide 'realistic' depictions of work or workers. Instead, they constitute what we might think of as an extensive, imaginative repertoire that Shakespeare draws on throughout his career and that he can use to establish dramatic tension and conflict, to build character, and to develop themes ranging from love to social order to violence to individual autonomy to national identity (to name just a few).

Let's return to *Henry V* and look at one example of a Shakespearian scene in which work is vividly invoked, but done so indirectly, through imagery and verbal reference. In what is perhaps his best-known speech in the play, King Henry gives a rousing address to rally his troops before the Battle of Agincourt, where the English were significantly outnumbered by their French rivals. The speech is often cited for its patriotism and rhetorical force, which raises the English soldiers' morale on the cusp of what initially appears to be an unwinnable battle. But this speech is also, at its core, a commentary on work, holiday, and national memory. Henry begins his speech as a direct response to a question about work: Warwick wishes aloud that they had with them 'But one ten thousand of those men in England | That do no work today' (4.3.17–18). Warwick imagines idle men at home who could instead be serving England on the battlefield in France. Henry responds with a quick dismissal: 'What's he that wishes so? | My cousin Warwick? No, my fair cousin. | If we are marked to die, we are enough | To do our country loss; and if to live, | The fewer men, the greater share of honour' (4.3.18–22). Henry then goes on to connect that honour to the specific feast day on which the battle occurs:

This day is called the Feast of Crispian.
He that outlives this day and comes safe home
Will stand a-tiptoe when this day is named
And rouse him at the name of Crispian. (4.3.40–3)

Henry's reference to Crispian clearly establishes the battle's place in the calendar (St Crispian's Day was traditionally celebrated on 25 October). But it also invokes the history behind the feast day itself: Saints Crispin and Crispianus were Roman brothers who worked as shoemakers and were martyred during the reign of Diocletian in the third century. As a result, they became the patron saints of shoemakers, and the Feast of Crispin was celebrated annually, with shoemakers' guilds taking a primary role in the festivities.

Through the reiterated reference to St Crispian, Henry's speech summons images of shoemakers in the midst of the battlefield. Why? One possible explanation, as Alison Chapman has suggested, is that 'because of their association with sturdy, well-built shoes, shoemakers were seen as good *foot* soldiers, and thus they stand for the ideal infantry which Harry will fling into battle'.[14] But this allusion can also help us interpret Henry's battlefield rhetoric and his role as a king and military leader. Henry invokes artisanal labour, here connected to an important feast day, for its nostalgic power, but also to broaden his audience beyond the elite lords on the battlefield: the allusion to shoemakers extends his community of supporters (whom he elsewhere in the speech memorably calls his 'band of brothers' [4.3.60]) beyond the nobility to include everyday citizens and workers. However, Henry creates this seemingly egalitarian sense of community through a rhetorical sleight of hand. He invokes shoemakers and their labour, but his main goal is to stir up patriotic sentiment, not highlight the lives of everyday workers. Effectively, Henry transforms this shoemaker's feast day into something else entirely: a day to celebrate military valour and create a collective memory that puts stirring feelings of patriotism in the service of the monarch and the nation, rather than of guilds or artisans. Nevertheless, even though Henry appropriates the work of shoemakers for his own political and military ends, that work is still crucial to the power of his speech.[15] This speech marks a pivotal moment in the play, and it is one that readers have often turned to in order to evaluate Henry's virtues and vices as a monarch and the play's complex presentation of warfare. But the force and complexity of the speech derive as much from its reference to St Crispian as it does to more expected images of battle. Henry's invocation of the feast day of shoemakers, in other words, figuratively brings that artisanal work and its cultural associations onto the stage and transforms them for visceral, dramatic effect. We can see, then, how even on the eve of battle, work can be a vital part of Shakespeare's stagecraft. By attending carefully not only to his plotting, but to the intricacies of his language and dramatic structure, we can more fully understand how Shakespeare's plays are influenced by the world of work.

Chapter Organization

The chapters that follow explore work from a variety of angles, drawing on examples from plays that span Shakespeare's career. In its aim to reach as broad a readership as possible, *Shakespeare and Work* does not assume detailed prior knowledge of working conditions in Shakespeare's England or in the theatre. The opening chapters provide this important context in addition to offering an overview of Shakespeare's own practices as a working playwright. The remaining chapters examine a range of plays from multiple genres (including many plays not typically 'read' in terms of work) and discuss several types of work either directly dramatized (e.g. service) or, more frequently, alluded to (e.g. agricultural work) in the plays. This book is not an exhaustive study of either Shakespeare or his representations of work. It does not, for instance, cover every example of a working character or allusion to labour in the plays, nor does it seek to provide a comprehensive understanding of the history of work in Shakespeare's England. It does, however, aim to be expansive in its reach, to offer a synthesis of important scholarship in the field, and to analyse a range of textual examples in order to elicit new understandings of the plays and encourage readers to pursue their own further study. In doing so, *Shakespeare and Work* reveals just how central the everyday world of work was to Shakespeare's dramatic practice.

Shakespeare and Work is divided into six chapters, in addition to this Introduction. Chapter 1, 'Shakespeare's World of Work', offers a brief history of working conditions and cultural attitudes towards work in Shakespeare's England. Historically, this was a key period of economic transition, as the gradual emergence of a capitalist economy in early modern England brought with it changing views about work, who should perform it, and what its social significance was. After providing an overview of these broader processes, the chapter then turns to examine the intimate connections between the early modern theatre and labour. Work is not just a topic explored in Shakespeare's plays; it was a vital component of the act of theatre-making itself. The English professional theatre was an economic institution that relied upon the labour of numerous people (actors, managers, playwrights, carpenters, costumers, and many others) to keep it running successfully. It was also a marketplace of ideas where debates about work, leisure, and the theatre's relationship to both were brought to life on stage. These debates, as we'll see throughout this book, animated many of the scenes, characters, and images in Shakespeare's plays.

The second chapter, 'Shakespeare as Working Artist', offers an overview of what there is to know about Shakespeare's work as a playwright—both in terms of his own practices as an author and how he was perceived by some early commentators. The chapter provides a survey of Shakespeare's writerly practices, including his engagement with his source material and his keen awareness of the playing companies and performance venues for which he was writing. The chapter will then consider how some of Shakespeare's earliest commentators, such as Ben Jonson, John Dryden, John Milton, and Samuel Johnson, wrote about Shakespeare as a working writer. Providing an overview of these early responses, this chapter will suggest that appreciating Shakespeare as a working artist is key to better understanding the centrality of work to his plays. Indeed, as the remainder of the book will explore, Shakespeare's plays themselves productively blur the dividing line between work and art.

The final four chapters of the book survey specific types of labour represented in Shakespeare's plays. These chapters begin with more overt, staged instances of work (Chapters 3 and 4) and then move to consider less obvious examples in which work is deployed structurally or metaphorically (Chapters 5 and 6). Chapter 3 ('Service and Domestic Work') examines service, with a primary focus on domestic service. Service is one of the most frequently represented forms of work in Shakespeare's plays, which feature numerous characters identified as servants and acting in that capacity during their onstage encounters.

Considering servant characters in plays such as *King Lear*, *Othello*, *Twelfth Night*, and *The Tempest*, this chapter provides an overview of the role of service work in Shakespeare's plays and demonstrates how service and servants significantly affect the dramatic structure of these texts. Particular attention is given to how Shakespeare addresses women's evolving position in the labour economy and to how his depictions of service and slavery were influenced by emerging understandings of race.

Chapter 4 ('Artisans and Apprentices') explores the role of artisans and apprentices in Shakespeare's plays and argues that his dramatization of these workers reveals a keen awareness of the social and economic contexts surrounding early modern craftspeople and their work. It discusses, for instance, how specific historical events, such as the 1596 uprisings of artisans and apprentices in England, influenced Shakespeare's treatment of craftspeople in his plays. Through readings of *Julius Caesar*, *Coriolanus*, *A Midsummer Night's Dream*, and *2 Henry VI*, this chapter invites us to consider not so much what Shakespeare 'thought' about artisans and other apprentices, but, more importantly, how these forms of work inform his characters and plots, including his staging of crowds and rebellion. It also looks beyond staged action to highlight how Shakespeare could deploy the language associated with apprentices and other manual labourers to draw attention to broader topics such as social order, violence, and even theatrical creativity.

In the book's final two chapters, we'll shift focus from work that is directly represented on stage to forms of work that appear in Shakespeare's drama via indirect reference or imagery. Chapter 5 ('Working the Green World') examines agricultural work, a form of labour that is almost never depicted directly on the early modern stage. Many of Shakespeare's plays that represent rural and agricultural settings have instead been discussed in terms of the 'green world', a concept that dates (at least in modern criticism) back to Northrop Frye's famous assessment of the forest or 'green world' as a 'symbol of natural society' in Shakespearian comedy.[16] This chapter will explore the ways in which labour remains resiliently present in the green world in ways we haven't fully accounted for. In addition to examining traditional 'green world' plays, such as *As You Like It* and *The Winter's*

Tale, this chapter will also consider in detail *Love's Labour's Lost*—a play rarely discussed in terms of either labour or the green world. As these readings will demonstrate, the structural rhythms of many green world comedies are established in and through images of agrarian labour.

Building on this discussion of green world labour, Chapter 6 ('Going to Market') examines the connections between more traditional forms of agricultural labour and the new kinds of work necessitated by a growing mercantile and capitalist economy. The chapter discusses how England's gradual transition to a capitalist economy during Shakespeare's lifetime, combined with its growing international engagements, changed understandings of work in fundamental ways. Shifts in attitudes and practices related to investment, credit, and commodity exchange, for instance, posed challenges to traditional concepts of labour, and the old and new often existed uneasily alongside each other. Examining plays such as *The Merchant of Venice*, *Macbeth*, *The Tempest*, and *The Merry Wives of Windsor*, this chapter explores how images of agricultural work in Shakespeare often function to justify or even romanticize newer, mercantile forms of labour. Agricultural work, that is, is not absent from these plays, just as it was not absent from the green worlds discussed in the previous chapter. Instead, we can trace how Shakespeare deploys images of rural cultivation and agricultural labour to help define and make sense of the newer and less tangible forms of work required of England's developing mercantile economy. Uncovering these connections can, in turn, reveal new interpretations of these plays.

The book concludes with an Epilogue ('Shakespeare's Working Words') that considers our own contemporary engagement with Shakespeare in the twenty-first century. It begins by contextualizing our current understanding of Shakespeare's relationship to work by looking back to some nineteenth-century responses to Shakespeare from members of the English and American working classes. Although critics and readers from earlier periods often read Shakespeare as purely a poet of the imagination, many readers in the Victorian period understood Shakespeare as allied to their radical political agendas and as a friend to working-class people. They thus interpreted Shakespeare as a 'popular' rather than an 'elite' artist. In our own contemporary moment, how might a fuller appreciation of Shakespeare's engagement with the world of work, as this book seeks to provide, affect how modern readers, students, and audiences approach his plays? The Epilogue argues that Shakespeare's working words offer a rich vantage point for exploring his impact on contemporary readers, including students in the secondary and post-secondary classrooms.

DOI: 10.1093/9780191998096.003.0001

1

Shakespeare's World of Work

What was the everyday world of work like in Shakespeare's England? This chapter will set the stage for the discussions that follow by providing a brief overview of the common types of work with which Shakespeare would have been familiar. In addition, it offers an overview of general working conditions in the period and a survey of cultural attitudes about work. We will begin by considering why the sixteenth and seventeenth centuries in England are a particularly important period within the broader history of work. By offering a brief history of the social, economic, and religious changes that characterized the period, we will trace how both the practices and ideas about work shifted in significant ways during Shakespeare's lifetime. The chapter will then explore in more detail several common types of work and how labour patterns shaped the lives of people at various social levels.[1] The final section of the chapter will highlight the specific relationship between labour and Shakespeare's theatre. We'll take a look at some of the heated debates from the period about the fundamental nature of theatre and consider how those debates might have influenced Shakespeare's own depictions of work in his plays.

Work and Change in Shakespeare's England

Working for wages was certainly not a new phenomenon in Shakespeare's lifetime. In England, wage labour had existed in some form for several hundreds of years before Shakespeare was born. And although the exact nature and timing of the transition between feudalism and capitalism are still much debated, it is undoubtedly true that this shift was under way well before the sixteenth century. The medieval period, for instance, 'witnessed the urban and commercial revolutions, the loosening of feudal ties, and the expansion of trade and industry based upon free labor'.[2] It is also true that several of the most dramatic events in the broader history of work and capitalist production occurred significantly *after* Shakespeare's lifetime. The technological advances that accompanied the Industrial Revolution beginning in the eighteenth century helped to establish capitalism as the dominant mode of production throughout Western Europe. By the time that he wrote and published the first volume of *Capital: A Critique of Political Economy* in the second half of the nineteenth century, Karl Marx could offer a robust and powerful critique of the capitalist system of production that identified the exploitation of human labour as its primary driving force.

Nevertheless, there were a number of significant socio-economic shifts that occurred during the sixteenth and seventeenth centuries that make the period surrounding Shakespeare's lifetime a particularly interesting one for investigating work. Indeed, Marx himself identified this period in English history as a key moment in the development of capitalism. Shakespeare was one of Marx's favourite writers, and he quotes frequently from the plays throughout his writing.[3] But in *Capital*, Marx also zeroes in on Shakespeare's England as a crucial period of economic change that would fundamentally affect labour practices. As Richard Halpern has argued, 'Marx takes England as the earliest and fullest example of capitalist development, and his historical exposition, which ranges from the sixteenth to the eighteenth centuries, focuses mainly on the ways in which a class of propertyless workers was produced.'[4] Essentially, Marx located in the early modern period in England the foundations of the capitalist mode of production; he saw the period as a kind of prelude to later developments. Near the end of volume I of *Capital*, for instance, he argues that although the beginnings of capitalist production can be seen as early as the fourteenth or the fifteenth centuries, what he calls the 'capitalist era' dates from the sixteenth century.[5] It is during Shakespeare's lifetime, in other words, that Marx identifies many of the key preconditions for later capitalist systems, including the gradual production of a dispossessed class of workers.

Marx offers a general template for understanding why the early modern period was significant in the history of work and to the development of wage labour specifically. But Marx's theoretical perspective can be supplemented and supported with more detailed evidence by considering some of the important historical changes that occurred during the sixteenth and seventeenth centuries in England. Indeed, we can turn to historical accounts of the period as well as to Shakespeare's own writings to better understand why and how attitudes towards work were changing. To begin with, let us back up a bit and consider how work was conceptualized in the period immediately predating Shakespeare's lifetime. In medieval England, society was commonly understood as a system of 'estates' divided into three parts: those who pray, those who fight, and those who labour. As John Wyclif wrote in *On the Duty of the King* (1378–9), 'It is clear that it is necessary for the parts of the kingdom to be coordinated in quantity and number, since if all were to be lords, who would be workers or servants?' Therefore, he concluded, 'it is necessary for there to be a three-fold hierarchy in the kingdom through which all are arranged into one person of one heart, namely, the priest or those who pray, the secular lords or defenders, and the common people or labourers'.[6] Work, according to this formulation, was the duty of only one of the three estates: the common labourers who formed the bottom of the hierarchy and who (in theory) supported the praying of the priests and the fighting of the nobility.

However, by the Elizabethan period, this model of the three estates was no longer the dominant one. 'The medieval assumption that work is the business only of one class of people,' as Tom Rutter notes, had largely 'vanished' by the sixteenth century.[7] In part, as we will see, this idea was replaced by a general expectation that all people have a duty to labour to avoid the sin of idleness. As a result, 'writers from the sixteenth century onward present non-manual occupations as forms of work'.[8] The early modern period thus gave rise to new ideas about labour that gradually took the place of the medieval model of the three estates. However, as is often the case, the divide between medieval and early modern was not an absolute one. As early as the twelfth century, England's growing urbanization and commercialization meant that the estates model was rapidly becoming incompatible with social and economic realities, even as it remained an important literary and philosophical theme.[9] Nor were Elizabethan assumptions about the duty to labour accepted by everyone. Many of the nobility, for instance, continued to assert their exemption from labour, or at least from manual labour.

Indeed, we can see the persistent influence of the medieval theory of the three estates in literature of the Elizabethan and Jacobean periods, including in Shakespeare's later plays. In Act 4 of *Cymbeline*, Belarius muses to himself about the princely attributes of his 'sons', Arviragus and Guiderius, the latter of which has just killed Cloten, son of the queen. In actuality, Arviragus and Guiderius are the two lost princes and heirs to the throne of Cymbeline, but since they have grown up in a mountain cave in Wales, raised by Belarius as his own sons, their heritage is as yet unknown to them. However, Belarius in this moment remarks on how the true nobility of these young men shines through, even if they remain unaware of it:

> 'Tis wonder
> That an invisible instinct should frame them
> To royalty unlearned, honour untaught,
> Civility not seen from other, valour
> That wildly grows in them, but yields a crop
> As if it had been sowed. (4.2.177–82)

As is frequently the case in Shakespeare, true nobility is hard to hide. But Belarius chooses a very specific metaphor here to describe this 'royalty unlearned, honour untaught.' He points out that their valour grows 'wildly' in them, meaning without cultivation or development. Nevertheless, it 'yields a crop | As if it had been sowed'. Arviragus and Guiderius thus produce the products of labour (the crop, in this case valour) without the actual work (the agricultural labour of sowing a field, or, in this case, developing valour through a royal upbringing at court). Belarius' agricultural metaphor invokes labour only to erase it. In the process, he emphasizes that true nobility is in fact established not through labour, but rather by being dissociated from it.

Shakespeare presents us with a similar moment in *The Winter's Tale* when Perdita, having been abandoned by her father, King Leontes, and raised by the Old Shepherd in Bohemia, appears at the sheep-shearing festival. The Old Shepherd scolds her, saying that she is acting more like someone who is 'retired' rather than the 'hostess of the meeting' (4.2.62, 64). He also compares her to his deceased wife, who used to perform the role of hostess with 'her face afire | With labour' and perform the duties of 'pantler, butler, cook, | Both dame and servant' (4.4.60, 56–7). Again, the text emphasizes Perdita's noble lineage by clearly distinguishing her from the Old Shepherd's labouring wife, who had approached the job of hostess as a series of discreet occupational duties. Perdita instead has to be taught to work in this capacity—it does not come naturally to her. As a gentleman in the Sicilian court will later describe it, Perdita possesses 'the affection of nobleness which nature shows above her breeding,' and that nobleness becomes visible in part through her discomfort with labour (5.2.36–7). We can glimpse in Belarius' speech and in the representation of Perdita, then, some powerful traces of the theory of the three estates, including the residual insistence that the nobility, in these examples, are defined explicitly as those who do not work.

But although the transition between medieval and early modern ideas about work was never a straightforward or seamless one, it remains the case that Shakespeare's lifetime was still a very important period of change in terms of theories and practices of labour. The late sixteenth and early seventeenth centuries in England witnessed a gradual, yet profound transition to new ways of understanding labour and the economy that would shape Shakespeare's plays in powerful ways. Several large-scale social and economic developments, for instance, transformed what it meant to work in Shakespeare's England. One of the most fundamental changes to England's labour force during this period was its dramatic increase in size. The population of England exploded during the sixteenth and seventeenth centuries, doubling between 1520 and 1680, when it reached about 5 million. The most rapid period of demographic growth occurred during the second half of the sixteenth century, and it was particularly acute in London, which saw its population more than double during that period, reaching around 150,000 by 1600.[10] In tandem with this growth in population, early modern England saw a substantial increase in trade and consumerism as English families became more dependent on goods produced outside the home, including imported goods brought in from overseas as a result of England's colonial practices and the growth of global trade routes. This rapidly expanding consumer economy combined with the sheer size of England's population both demanded and produced a larger, more diverse workforce. Many of those workers were drawn away from agricultural regions to urban centres, especially London. Because intense population growth put additional pressure on the land, as some regions struggled to maintain their newly expanded populations, the period witnessed a dramatic increase in geographical mobility and a gradual redistribution of England's population towards towns and urban areas.

England's explosive population growth had additional effects on labour as well. Inflation rose substantially between the 1570s and the 1630s, in part because the expanding population was putting increased pressure on England's comparatively inelastic food resources. Wages, by contrast, rose less quickly than prices, which meant that the real wages of labourers declined significantly during this same period.[11] As a result of England's demographic growth, then, workers' wages remained low, and unemployment (or underemployment) was an ongoing reality. At the same time, a much greater percentage of the English population was dependent on wages for their livelihood by the time of Shakespeare's death in 1616 than in 1564, when he was born. By some estimates, almost half of the population was dependent either partially or solely on wages by the middle of the seventeenth century.[12] As historian Keith Wrightson summarizes, structural characteristics such as demographic growth and the dependence upon wage labour were not in and of themselves new in the sixteenth and seventeenth centuries. Rather, what had changed was 'the proportion of the population whose domestic economies were structured by such realities,' with the result that 'the wage-dependent population had expanded and diversified' significantly within Shakespeare's lifetime.[13]

In addition to these socio-economic changes, the Protestant Reformation also created new understandings of work and its value. Without exaggerating the causal relationship, it seems fair to say that Protestant believers could find in the new doctrines of Luther, Calvin, and others a 'framework in which manual and commercial work could be favourably represented'.[14] In particular, the Protestant doctrine of vocations (or callings) critiqued the Catholic monastic system for idleness and redefined labour not as a punishment for sin, but as a positive virtue and a means to salvation.[15] In *1 Henry IV*, we see Falstaff jokingly reference this new understanding of work as vocation in an exchange with Hal prior to the robbery at Gadshill. After Hal observes that Falstaff has changed his tune from 'praying to purse-taking',

Falstaff responds: 'Why, Hal, 'tis my vocation, Hal. 'Tis no sin for a man to labour in his vocation' (1.2.103–5). Comically equating theft with a legitimate 'vocation,' Falstaff justifies his behaviour by pointing to the new, post-Reformation understanding of work not as sinful idleness, but as a sanctioned path to redemption. And although, of course, his application of this doctrine wildly misses the mark, Falstaff nevertheless assumes that Hal will agree with the basic equation (work=vocation=virtue) that underwrites his joke.

As well as highlighting the virtue inherent in labour, the post-Reformation emphasis on vocation also enabled forms of non-manual labour to be redefined as valuable work. The medieval three estates system, as we've seen, emphasized that nobles were those who fought rather than worked. In the sixteenth and seventeenth centuries, however, the processes of state formation as well as changes in warfare meant that the military endeavours of nobles were less significant than they had previously been. The focus, instead, shifted to nobles as labouring in public office, through the 'vocation' of government. Humanist philosophers of the period shared this general understanding of labour: excess leisure or inactivity was to be avoided at all costs and instead the *vita activa* (the active life) was held up as a glorified ideal.[16] The main connecting thread here is the rejection of idleness and a heightened sense of work as a social good that must be undertaken (in some form) by *all*—not just by members of one rank of society.

This new emphasis on work as a universal duty is perhaps most famously articulated in the Homily Against Idleness, one of the twenty-one new homilies added to the 1563 Book of Homilies, which was first published in 1547. The Homily opens with a clear statement about the dangers of idleness and the virtues of honest labour:

> Forasmuch as man, being not born to ease and rest, but to labour and travail, is by corruption of nature through sin so far degenerated and grown out of kind that he taketh idleness to be no evil at all, but rather a commendable thing, seemly for those that be wealthy, and therefore is greedily embraced of most part of men, as agreeable to their sensual affection and all labour and travail is diligently avoided as a thing painful and repugnant to the pleasure of the flesh, it is necessary to be declared unto you that by the ordinance of God which he hath set in the nature of man, everyone ought, in his lawful vocation and calling, to give himself to labour, and that idleness, being repugnant to the

same ordinance, is a grievous sin, and also, for the great inconveniences and mischiefs which spring thereof, an intolerable evil; to the intent that when you understand the same you may diligently flee from it and on the other part earnestly apply yourselves, every man in his vocation, to honest labour and business, which as it is enjoined unto man by God's appointment, so it wanteth not his manifold blessings and sundry benefits.[17]

Labour should not be understood as a 'painful and repugnant' task; rather, honest labour, pursued in terms of a 'lawful vocation and calling', will lead to many spiritual blessings and benefits. This shift from the idea that work is a burden of only a subset of the population to the widespread belief that work is expected of all is one of the most profound changes to the understanding of labour that occurred in Shakespeare's lifetime. In early modern England, then, work had come to be recognized as a pervasive element of all aspects of society. Taken together with the other socio-economic changes we have briefly surveyed here, this development meant that work was a hot topic for discussion, debate, and dramatization on Shakespeare's stage.

Working Lives

What were the daily lives of working people like in Shakespeare's England? What kind of work did people do, and how did it affect how they saw themselves as individuals? While it is challenging to generalize across the period, given the variations between regions, workers of different social ranks, and diverse forms of employment, we can sketch some broad strokes about people's working lives in early modern England. Work was a central part of early modern culture, and for most people, especially people at the lower and middle ranks of society, that made for a life that was defined by a great deal of difficult toil and little time for leisure. We can see this mapped out in the 1563 Elizabethan Statute of Artificers, a set of regulations that brought together and codified a varied set of labour laws that dated back to the Middle Ages.[18] Among other things, the Statute stipulated how long workers should labour each day. Describing the season between March and September, for instance, it set forth that 'all artificers and labourers being hired for wages by the day or week shall', during this part of the year:

be and continue at their work, at or before five of the clock in the morning, and continue at work, and not depart, until between seven and eight of the clock at night (except it be in the time of breakfast, dinner or drinking, the which times at most shall not exceed two and a half hours in a day, that is to say, at every drinking one half-hour, for his dinner, one hour, and for his sleep, when he is allowed to sleep, the which is from the midst of May, to the midst of August, half an hour at the most, and at every breakfast one half-hour).[19]

Centuries before the five-day workweek became standard, working days were generally long and often exceedingly difficult. And, at least according to the Statute, the general expectation was that there would be a degree of consistency in work effort, a daily routine that would be repeated over time.

In practice, however, there was more variability than the formalized and didactic language of the Statute suggests. If we broaden our focus out from an individual day to consider a broader temporal spectrum, we find much greater irregularity within early modern cultures of work. Although the goal of the Statute of Artificers was to codify and standardize labour practices in the period, most work in Shakespeare's England resisted categorization and was instead highly variable over the course of a season, a year, or a lifetime. The Statute, for example, attempted to control and limit the mobility of workers by, for instance, levying stiff penalties for employees who left work (whether day labour or a longer term of service) before their contracted time was completed. Nevertheless, most historical evidence suggests that labour throughout this period was more likely to be characterized by geographical and occupational mobility rather than stasis. Work, especially at the lower social levels, was often intermittent and seasonal, a fact that we can glimpse in the Statute's own reference to working patterns between 'March and September' as compared with the rest of the year. The inconsistency of work patterns was common to most working people in the period, but it was especially true for women. Indeed, precisely because of the temporary and discontinuous nature of much of their work, early modern women at all social levels were more likely than men to participate in multiple sectors of the labour economy over the course of their lives.

Work, even for wages, often began at a young age, for both boys and girls. Especially in rural settings, children would start working when they were as young as 10 or 11. Initially, most of this work would occur within their parents' household, with younger children in agricultural communities given tasks such as 'fetching water and milk, gathering sticks for fuel, bringing food to those working the fields', or attending to animal husbandry.[20] Older children would typically be given more demanding tasks, such as assisting with harvesting or ploughing. This work remained largely piecemeal and casual, as was true for much of early modern society. By the time children reached their middle teens and early adult years, they likely separated from their family home and began to work elsewhere. Often, they worked as servants in the households of other families, something we will discuss in more detail in Chapter 3. But in addition to domestic service, they also entered careers ranging from mercantile trades and urban crafts to service in husbandry.[21] And many continued to work multiple jobs either simultaneously or over the course of their lives. Even yeomen, who were typically agricultural workers who owned and farmed a fairly substantial acreage of land, often worked jobs other than farming in order to maintain their livelihoods. As Alexandra Shepard has demonstrated, yeomen during this period also worked in such occupations as 'baker, maltster, malt-dealer, gardener, grazier, brewer, tailor, grocer, chandler, innkeeper, scrivener, schoolmaster, and parish clerk', among others.[22] For many people in Shakespeare's England, then, their working lives were both difficult and varied, marked often by a multiplicity of occupations and geographical disjunctions.

We get a vivid glimpse of the instability and variety that characterized many working lives in the period in the character of Sly in *The Taming of the Shrew.* In the play's Induction, a lord and his huntsmen find the lowborn Christopher Sly intoxicated and sleeping on the ground and decide to trick him into believing that he is a lord, hiring a group of travelling players to perform the subsequent *Taming of the Shrew* for his entertainment. Sly adamantly defines himself in terms of his status as a lower-order labourer. In response to being addressed as 'your honor' and praised as a 'mighty man,' Sly retorts: 'What, would you make me mad? Am not I Christopher Sly—old Sly's son of Burton Heath, by birth a pedlar, by education a cardmaker, by transmutation a bearherd, and now by present profession a tinker?' (Induction 2.12, 13, 16–20). Sly defines himself through a series of occupational positions, resisting the fanciful terms hoisted upon him by the lords and instead attempting to define his identity by listing the types of work with which he has been associated. Notably, Sly identifies himself with a range of occupations over time, including stints as a pedlar of wares and as a cardmaker, a maker of metal combs used in preparing wool for spinning. Although his 'present profession' as a tinker, a mender of pots and other household items, seems to offer a suitable telos to his occupational history, his speech suggests that future professions may very well supplant this present one, just as it has supplanted others in turn. Sly thus in many ways represents the quintessential itinerant worker of the period who would have performed multiple jobs over the course of a lifetime.

But Shakespeare also suggests that Sly's occupational instability correlates with disorderly behaviour in need of regulation, a role comically filled by the lord and his huntsmen in the Induction. The presence of large numbers of temporary labourers in early modern England led to concerns about social order, concerns that were based in part on the belief that displaced labour was not legitimate work. As we have seen, the Statute of Artificers attempted to regulate labour in an effort to maintain social order, but apprehensions about itinerancy and vagrancy (which we will return to in the next section of this chapter) remained high throughout the period. Indeed, pedlars and tinkers—the trades that bookend Sly's catalogue of employment—were occupations specifically designated as illegal in the vagrancy acts of 1572 and 1598.[23] Sly's labour history thus marks him as potentially unstable and disorderly; he inhabits a range of transitory occupations that could carry connotations of vagrancy, poverty, and social instability. This is certainly how the lord and his huntsmen respond to Sly when they find him: they identify him as a lowly figure of disorder, a 'drunken man' and a 'beggar' rather than as a worker, the terms with which Sly identifies himself. By emphasizing Sly's confusion over his own social status as he is temporarily removed from one social world and elevated to another, these different perspectives on Sly's occupational positions help shape the comedic force of the play's opening scenes. At the same time, they also draw attention to the complex relationships between work, identity, and social order in the period.

Most workers in Shakespeare's England would have held many jobs throughout their lives, but they nevertheless often developed a sense of occupational identity, much as we see in Sly's catalogue of employments. Indeed, historians have demonstrated that early modern England witnessed a gradual shift 'whereby occupational identity became increasingly bound up with what people *did* for a living, rather than what they *had* on which to depend.'[24] Social classification, in other words, was becoming more about occupation as an 'activity and set of skills required to generate income' rather than about one's estate.[25] Even when it was temporary rather than stable, work offered many people access to a form of self-understanding that enabled them to define their personal worth in terms that were not exclusively financial, but also tied to other, more intangible forms of value.[26] Shakespeare's drama was ideally positioned to play a vital role in this process of socio-economic change. By staging working characters and giving voice to a wide range of perspectives on occupation and labour, Shakespeare's plays help shift how work itself was imagined, and how new understandings of work as identity (for instance) could become conceptually possible over time.

We can see a powerful invocation of the idea of occupation in *Othello*. In the pivotal Act 3, scene 3, Othello becomes convinced by Iago of Desdemona's infidelity. Tormented by his jealousy, Othello also sees the moment as a turning point in his own life, one in which his former duties as a soldier no longer retain their force over his identity:

> O now for ever
> Farewell the tranquil mind, farewell content,
> Farewell the plumèd troops and the big wars
> That makes ambition virtue! O, farewell,
> The spirit-stirring drum, th'ear-piercing fife,
> The royal banner, and all quality,
> Pride, pomp, and circumstance of glorious war!
> And O, you mortal engines whose rude throats
> Th'immortal Jove's dread clamours counterfeit,
> Farewell! Othello's occupation's gone. (3.3.352–62)

Othello laments the loss of a vital part of his self-identity: his occupation as a soldier. He attributes his 'tranquil mind' and feelings of 'content' to his military labours and all the physical as well as emotional experiences that accompanied them. All of this has been shattered by his belief that his own marriage and domestic life are under threat.

But even as this speech announces a clear turn in the play towards revenge and domestic tragedy (rather than military exploits), it also offers a compelling example of the growing connection between work and individual identity. Work, understood positively in terms of vocation, was intimately connected with individual reputation and social credit in post-Reformation England. We see this vividly in *Othello*, as Othello concludes that his own loss of occupation affects his personal and social standing in the play, even though his actual rank or status remains unchanged. As we will continue to see throughout this book, Shakespeare's plays are creative and often provocative mediums for investigating the working lives of early modern people and for bringing changing (and sometimes conflicting) ideas about labour to vivid life on stage.

Work and Shakespeare's Theatre

Work was a topic explored in Shakespeare's plays, but it was also a vital component of the act of theatre-making itself. In addition to the social and economic changes that we've already traced in this chapter, significant developments in theatrical practice and management during Shakespeare's lifetime dramatically transformed the relationship between work and the stage. Identifying these changes as well as the debates and challenges they produced will help us establish some of the immediate, theatrical contexts in which Shakespeare was writing, enabling us to better understand why work was such a charged and vital subject of exploration on the Shakespearian stage.

The last few decades of the sixteenth century in England witnessed several significant developments that directly affected the economic position of the early modern theatre. Although professional actors and entertainers can be traced back as early as the fifteenth century, most acting prior to the late sixteenth century in England was performed as an 'avocation, undertaken intermittently and in off-hours by people whose main source of income lay elsewhere'.[27] But this began to change as the civic drama, such as the mystery plays, which were traditionally linked to religious holidays and festivals, declined in popularity in the sixteenth century. Touring companies of players, initially affiliated with monarchs and the nobility, began to take their place. These groups performed on days of the week not limited to religious holidays, and their members were often individuals who did not necessarily have other sources of income. This shift was even more pronounced in London, which saw the building of purpose-built, permanent playhouses in the 1570s, including the Theatre in Shoreditch in 1576.[28] The professional playing companies that took advantage of these new venues for performance heralded a new era in which theatre became both an immensely popular art form and also big business.

The professional theatre in Shakespeare's day was, as Walter Cohen has argued, a 'fundamentally artisanal historical form'.[29] We can see this especially in the organization of the professional playing companies, which are best understood as hybrid or transitional entities that retained many of the structures of the medieval guilds, while also taking advantage of new and innovative forms of commercial enterprise. Like the London craft guilds, the playing companies were communal and collaborative endeavours, and they retained the apprenticeship system common to the guilds. By preserving these kinds of guild structures, the newly developed playing companies of the late sixteenth century connected the labour of acting directly to that of the artisanal crafts, helping to justify their novel endeavours in the process.[30] At the same time, the Elizabethan playing companies were also typically structured on the joint-stock model. In this system, a 'nucleus of committed members would organize themselves both theatrically and financially into an entity, to secure both patronage and a patent and to share costs and profits'. Typically, there would be eight to ten principal men who served as the 'sharers' in the company. Shakespeare, for instance, was listed as a sharer in the royal patent that established the new King's Men acting company (formerly known as the Lord Chamberlain's Men) in 1603.[31]

Acting companies in Shakespeare's England were thus structured according to both older guild structures and newer commercial models. They also depended upon a wide range of different kinds of workers to mount and ensure the success of their performances. High-level carpenters, painters, and textile workers, for instance, were needed to support professional theatrical production, and this demand only grew across the period as the professional theatres increased in number and popularity. Over the course of the sixteenth and seventeenth centuries, 'a regular population of theater craftspeople emerges', a development that 'points to the existence of a body of skills and techniques that actors, producers, and playwrights would have both known of and been able to depend on in their work'.[32] In addition, more informal networks of workers supplied a range of goods and services that directly supported the London public theatres. Women were a vital part of these networks, manufacturing costumes and properties, working as gatherers (collecting admission fees for the theatres), and participating in the growing credit economy of the period through their work as moneylenders and pawnbrokers.[33] The commercial theatres in Shakespeare's London were intimately connected to the broader labour economy of the city, and they relied upon the work of numerous men and women both inside and outside the walls of the playhouses to stage their plays and keep their businesses afloat.

Along with these developments in the English professional theatre came an understanding of actors themselves as workers. This was true in two senses. First, many actors began their working lives within the larger London economy outside the theatres. Second, when they joined a playing company, these actors were increasingly viewed *as workers* by playwrights and other company members. Although over the course of Shakespeare's lifetime the theatre would become a more and more viable source of income and professional stability for many people, including actors, playwrights, company sharers, and the many skilled labourers who produced goods for theatrical productions, many of those who would go on to become actors in the professional playing companies began their careers in other professions entirely. As David Kathman's archival research makes clear, many professional players in Elizabethan London were freemen (meaning that they were members of livery companies, such as the Goldsmiths or the Grocers). And although we might assume that 'the occupation of a freeman and his apprentices necessarily corresponded to his livery company—that a freeman of the Goldsmiths, for example, must have made his living working with gold and must have trained his apprentices in that craft', this was not in fact the case. As Kathman demonstrates, 'freemen were under no obligation to practice the trades of their companies, and a substantial minority made their living in other ways', including in the professional theatres. The London livery companies thus 'played a crucial role in the economics of the professional theatre, particularly its apprenticeship system'.[34] There was, in other words, a direct pipeline between London's livery companies and the professional theatres.

Once they joined playing companies, actors also developed strong commercial and working bonds with their fellow players that highlighted their status as both players and workers. While the guild model upon which theatrical companies were based necessitated hierarchal divisions and uneven distributions of power, this did not preclude the development of strong fraternal bonds among actors and a 'sense of professional community' that helped facilitate the 'development of cooperative commercial strategies that accommodated change and promoted growth' in the early modern theatre.[35] Furthermore, many late sixteenth-century plays, as Tom Rutter has demonstrated, make a concerted effort to depict acting as work rather than idleness. In the first scene of the Induction of *The Taming of the Shrew*, for instance, Shakespeare depicts a group of touring actors, who are praised by the Lord for their skill:

> LORD This fellow I remember
> Since once he played a farmer's eldest son.
> 'Twas where you wooed the gentlewoman so well.
> I have forgot your name, but sure that part
> Was aptly fitted and naturally performed.
> ANOTHER PLAYER I think 'twas Soto that your honour means.
> LORD 'Tis very true. Thou didst it excellent. (81–7)

Here, the Lord acknowledges the actors for their professionalism, and for work that is accomplished and worthy of praise. Even though these are itinerant players, the focus in this exchange is not on their status as potential rogues or vagabonds, but rather their position as legitimate, trained professionals.[36]

In plays from the last few decades of the sixteenth century, we see similar assertions on the part of Shakespeare and other playwrights. In part, these representations are a pointed response to antitheatricalists and other critics who often seized on the connection between actors and vagrancy to attack the theatre as an institution. As we saw in the previous section, despite the attempts of the Statute of Artificers to control labourers in order to maintain stability and social order, the Vagrancy Acts of 1572 and 1598 reiterated the concerns of many authorities about vagrancy in the period. Antitheatricalist treatises, typically written by preachers, political authorities, and other moralists, condemned the theatre as a place that encouraged moral laxity and social disorder. But they also specifically attacked the theatre as a space of idleness, a place where work was notably absent. Preacher John Northbrooke, for instance, argues broadly that Satan works through theatres to corrupt humans. But he also positions theatres as the antithesis of work, claiming forthrightly that 'more Idleness can there not be, than where such plays and interludes are'.[37] William Rankins complains that plays transform audience members so that they no longer remember 'the profitable fruits of virtuous labor'. The players, he laments, 'do not only exercise themselves in all kind of idleness, but minister occasion to many to incur the like'.[38] The public theatre, according to these tracts, was both the product and the source of idleness, luring people away from virtuous labour and proper occupations.

Many antitheatricalist writers attacked the players more directly and drew a strict contrast between acting and work. Philip Stubbes, for example, described actors as 'a great sort of idle persons, doing nothing but playing and loitering, having their livings of the sweat of other men's brows, much like unto drones devouring the sweet honey of the poor laboring bees'. He later describes traveling players as 'rogues and vagabonds,' an explicit reference to the 1563 Statute of Artificers.[39] In *Plays Confuted in Five Actions* (1582) Stephen Gosson attacks the players at length and alleges that many actors are 'men of occupations, which they have forsaken to live by playing'—drawing yet another contrast between other (legitimate) sites of employment and the theatre. Gosson goes on to remind his readers about the importance of the Christian concept of vocation and argues that actors have essentially abandoned this duty. 'We are commanded by God to abide in the same calling wherein we were called, which is our ordinary vocation in a commonweal,' he states. 'Let them not,' he concludes, 'look to live by plays.'[40] In addition to asserting that acting took people away from their lawful vocations, antitheatricalists also emphasized the connection between the stage and idleness by linking theatre to another antithesis of work: sleep. In *The School of Abuse* (1579), for example, Gosson insists that not only have players fallen 'from just labor to unjust idleness', but also that the theatre insidiously leads playgoers 'to pleasure, sloth, sleep, sin'.[41] Once again, the theatre is sinful because it is a source of idleness, and also because it is affiliated with sloth and excessive sleep, behaviours that are impediments to disciplined labour. Similar themes were frequently articulated by these and other polemical writers, but they were also reiterated more officially in late sixteenth-century legal documents such as the Act of the Court of Aldermen (dated between 1582 and 1587) and the 1597 Lord Mayor's letter to the Privy Council, which denounced actors as idle vagrants and rogues. Collectively, these texts respond to the purpose-built professional theatres and regular performances coming to characterize the late sixteenth-century English stage by arguing that 'the theatre is bad for business', luring apprentices, servants, and other workers away from legitimate sites of labour.[42]

The theatre in Shakespeare's England was thus a crucial site of debate about the nature of work in the period. As the heated arguments of the antitheatricalist writers demonstrate, many of these debates focused in particular on the professional actor's status as a worker (or not) and sought to define acting in relation to work, leisure, and idleness. As such, the theatre consolidated and amplified many of the socio-economic concerns about labour that we've traced throughout this chapter. In doing so, it became an especially important site for publicly and creatively reimagining how work was understood in early modern England. The economic institution that was the English professional theatre was, in other words, both a place of work in its own right as well as a marketplace of ideas where debates about the nature of work and leisure could be staged. Of course, Shakespeare and other playwrights from the period did not simply accept the largely negative antitheatricalist judgements that maintained that work and theatre were diametrically opposed to each other. Occasionally, they responded to such attacks directly, even by writing their own defences of the theatre, as playwright Thomas Heywood did in his *An Apology for Actors* in 1612. More commonly, they responded through the fictional worlds and dramatic language of their plays. And this, as the rest of this book demonstrates, is precisely what Shakespeare did. Shakespeare takes the vexed, highly charged, and timely topic of work and weaves it into the fabric of his plays. By attending to Shakespeare's engagement with the early modern world of work, then, we can come to a richer understanding of his dramatic output as it continues to influence generations of readers and audiences.

Shakespeare and Work. Michelle M. Dowd, Oxford University Press. © Michelle M. Dowd 2026.
DOI: 10.1093/9780191998096.003.0002

2

Shakespeare as Working Artist

As we saw in the previous chapter, the theatres in Shakespeare's day were themselves workplaces. Acting companies and the performers they employed were part of a dynamic and culturally significant business enterprise that was both enormously successful and, in part due to that success, the focus of critique and heated debate. But what do we know about Shakespeare's own work as a writer for that theatre? This chapter discusses Shakespeare's work as a playwright, both in terms of his background as an actor and theatre professional and in terms of his writerly processes, including his reading and treatment of source materials. It also briefly explains how the work of early modern printers supported and supplemented Shakespeare's own work as a writer by enabling the appearance of his plays as printed texts. The final section of the chapter considers how some of the earliest commentators on Shakespeare wrote about him as a working writer. Although many early writers praised Shakespeare's 'natural' talent and suggested his poetic genius was a result of him *not* working too hard at writing, others, notably Ben Jonson, took the opposite approach and linked his artistic endeavours directly with work. And although it wasn't immediately embraced by other critics, Jonson's position is strongly supported by the available cultural and theatrical evidence we have about Shakespeare's work as a playwright, as this chapter as a whole demonstrates. For Shakespeare, in other words, art and work were inseparable.

Shakespeare as Actor and Theatrical Professional

Shakespeare wrote for the theatre not as an outsider, but as someone who had been deeply embedded within theatrical culture for most of his adult life. He began his theatrical career as an actor, although exactly how he got his start as a player is 'the stuff of myth rather than veritable fact'.[1] From the christening of his twin children, Hamnet and Judith, in 1585 until Robert Greene refers to him as an 'upstart crow' within London's theatrical scene in 1592, the historical record on Shakespeare's life is a virtual blank. This gap in the record has prompted numerous speculations as to what Shakespeare might have been up to, during a period generally referred to by his biographers as the 'Lost Years'. One common speculation is that he joined a group of actors and toured the provinces during this time, eventually becoming a member of the Queen's Men, a company formed by Queen Elizabeth and Sir Francis Walsingham primarily for touring—a kind of mobile advertisement for the Queen's generosity.[2] After his move to London in the 1590s, Shakespeare seems to have made a gradual transition from actor to playwright, although once again the precise timing of that transition is impossible to pin down. As John Astington notes: 'He may have been a member of Strange's, Pembroke's and Sussex's companies between 1592 and 1594' and he seems to have been 'among the founding group of the Chamberlain's men in 1594'.[3] We also know that he acted in several plays by Ben Jonson, notably *Every Man in His Humour* in 1598, *Every Man out of His Humour* in 1599, and *Sejanus* in 1603 (where he appeared second on the list of actors, after Richard Burbage).[4] Jonson seems to have considered Shakespeare to be an actor worthy of some note, but in general Shakespeare was far better known for his skills as a playwright than for his acting talents. Nevertheless, his work as an actor directly informed his work as a playwright, as did his extensive experience with the theatre more broadly.

However little we may know about the specific details of Shakespeare's acting career, we can state with certainty that he wrote his plays as a man of the theatre, a position he secured through his decades-long involvement with individual actors, acting companies, and theatrical venues. Shakespeare bought a share of the Lord Chamberlain's Men company in 1594, and he would remain with the company (which later became the King's Men in 1603 on the ascension of James I to the throne after Elizabeth's death) for the rest of his career. His association with this company helped support his work as a writer in at least two ways. First, as a longstanding sharer in the company, Shakespeare benefited from an unusually high degree of professional security that in turn afforded him a great deal of financial security over time. As Janet Dillon notes, Shakespeare was unusual in that he wrote plays for only a single company and did so from such an early date in his career.[5] When the Globe theatre was built in 1599 out of the timbers from the original Theatre, Shakespeare was one of ten players (called 'housekeepers') who bought shares to finance the new theatre's construction. By 1605, these two sources of revenue (his shares in the company and in the playhouse) were bringing Shakespeare some handsome financial profits, enough so that he was able to buy several properties in his hometown of Stratford. Shakespeare's work in the theatre and his status as a shareholder, in other words, was his primary source of livelihood, and it enabled his career as a playwright to flourish over several decades.[6]

Second, Shakespeare's lengthy collaboration with the Lord Chamberlain's/King's Men meant that he was quite familiar with the company's performance practices and with the specific actors who would take parts in his plays. London commercial theatres operated on a repertory system, which meant that companies performed a different play every day, with the typical exceptions of Sundays, Lent, and major church holidays. New plays were introduced to the rotation approximately every three weeks. As a result, '[p]reparations had to move at high speed, with new plays going into production within about three weeks of the script being purchased and actors learning new parts while continuing to perform their existing repertory of roles'.[7] In addition, the nature of the repertory system meant that companies had to stage a large and diverse group of plays that would appeal to the changing tastes of theatrical audiences. As Roslyn Knutson has demonstrated, the Chamberlain's Men's repertoire in the 1590s, for instance, included a diverse range of genres, including revenge tragedy, romantic tragedy, and a variety of types of comedy. It also featured the immensely popular history plays, which 'illustrate the opportunity of the repertory system to market plays as sequels and serials'.[8] The result was a complex, multifaceted, and cooperative workforce in which playwrights could 'readily supply scripts on popular topics in fashionable genres that were marketable on stage'.[9] Shakespeare's own extensive theatrical experience would have ensured that he understood this system inside and out, and he would have written his plays with the marketing and artistic concerns of the company in mind. Shakespeare's decision to write history plays in the 1590s, for example, was not a decision made in artistic isolation; rather, it was a decision made in conjunction with his company and in full knowledge of the commercial aspects of theatre that directly affected such things as popularity, audience tastes, and the need for a diversity of offerings if the company was going to thrive.

Another common aspect of the repertory system that directly affected Shakespeare's work as a writer was the use of 'parts' or 'cue scripts'. Unlike today, when actors are likely to receive the entire script of a play in which they will be performing, Shakespeare's actors typically only received their individual parts on a roll of paper. The roll would contain all of that actor's lines and a short cue (usually the last few words of the speech that came immediately before)—nothing more. Certainly, such a system would have had a profound influence on how actors learned their roles and on how early modern plays were performed. But it also shaped Shakespeare's own craft as a playwright. Being thoroughly familiar with the part-script as the fundamental unit out of which plays were constructed, Shakespeare wrote his characters and their individual speeches with this technology at the forefront of his mind. So, for instance, given the heightened importance of the cue and its placement in the text, Shakespeare tended to put 'anything of permanent importance to the play' at the end of speeches and, thus, in the cue.[10] Careful attention to part-scripts and cues was fundamental to Shakespeare's creative artistry, shaping how he fashioned characters and how he wrote speeches and dialogue.

As part of this process, Shakespeare would also tailor particular roles to specific actors. Shakespeare's long-term association with the Lord Chamberlain's/King's Men meant that he knew the individual actors who would take his parts. As a result, Shakespeare and his company actors together formed a working team that helped to shape the dramatic stories that he told. This kind of collaborative work is traceable in the nuances of Shakespeare's characterizations of individual parts, which reflect a personal awareness of the talents (and limitations) of specific actors. As Simon Palfrey and Tiffany Stern describe Shakespeare's writing process, 'Even as he was meditating upon some brand new work, deep within the fabled smithy of his imagination, part of the metal must have been his mates, their jokes or aura or expectations, the voices from the previous day's playing or the night's carousing. So he shaped each written part to a particular actor.'[11] Once again, Shakespeare's artistic process was never an isolated one, but one built in and through theatrical community; his plays were directly influenced by the personalities and skills of the actors who would ultimately bring them to life. Shakespeare's plays are what they are 'because of the players who first played them'.[12]

We can see this synergy between playwright and actor at work in Shakespeare's creation of clowns and leading comedic roles early in his writing career. In the 1590s, the Lord Chamberlain's Men were fortunate to have the talented and well-known comedian William Kempe in their company. He was likely the most famous member of the company at the time, and Shakespeare wrote several notable comedic roles for him: Launce in *The Two Gentlemen of Verona*, Bottom in *A Midsummer Night's Dream*, Launcelot Gobbo in *The Merchant of Venice*, and Dogberry in *Much Ado About Nothing*, among others. But Kempe wasn't just a funny man; he seems to have had distinctive comedic skills that Shakespeare took advantage of when writing these characters. As Lucy Munro notes, the characters played by Kempe 'manipulate and deform language through puns, wordplay, and malapropism; much of their comedy derives from moments at which plain-speaking men of lower social status are brought into contact with the practices and pretensions of the elite'.[13] Shakespeare drew upon Kempe's specific comedic talents when crafting these characters, what we might think of as a kind of theatrical collaboration between playwright and actor. Knowing that he was writing for Kempe changed how Shakespeare wrote.

In 1599 the Lord Chamberlain's Men acquired a new comedic actor to replace Kempe: Robert Armin. Armin had a notably different comedic style than Kempe. He was more sardonic, wry, and known for his singing and lute playing (whereas Kempe had been well known for his dancing). Although Armin did take on the comedic roles previously played by Kempe in the company's repertory, he also developed new roles that had different characteristics from those of his predecessor.

The so-called 'wise' fools that Shakespeare created for the company after 1600, including the Fool in *King Lear*, Touchstone in *As You Like It*, Feste in *Twelfth Night*, and Lavatch in *All's Well that Ends Well*, were all written with Armin in mind. These roles were often 'professional court fools' who typically 'voice a satiric perspective that is more wry and knowing' than that of Kempe's characters.[14] Once again, we can connect a shift in Shakespeare's writerly process to his intimate working knowledge of the actors who would be taking on his roles. Furthermore, understanding how Shakespeare worked as a playwright can help explain why some characters (such as the 'wise' fool) 'seem to exist in more than one play'. Hamlet alludes to this kind of typecasting among professional actors in his conversation with Rosencrantz and Guildenstern about the arrival of the traveling players:

> He that plays the King shall be welcome; his majesty shall have tribute of me. The adventurous Knight shall use his foil and target, the Lover shall not sigh gratis, the Humorous Man shall end his part in peace, the Clown shall make those laugh whose lungs are tickled o'th' sear, and the Lady shall say her mind freely, or the blank verse shall halt for't. (2.2.321–8)

Hamlet identifies the as-yet unmet actors according to the kinds of roles they typically play, creating a taxonomy that links individual plays to specific dramatic roles (Figure 2.1). As Tiffany Stern suggests, this phenomenon of 'across-play types' is directly 'traceable to actors' personalities'.[15] Many of Shakespeare's most famous characters, in other words, were the result of his collective creative work as a long-standing member of an active playing company.

We can see another example of the synergy between Shakespeare's works and the characteristics or skills of individual actors in the revision of specific character parts across different texts of the same play. In *Othello*, for instance, Desdemona sings in the 1623 Folio text, but not in the 1622 Quarto. In Act 4 of the play, alone with Emilia as she prepares for bed, Desdemona in the Folio sings the 'willow' song:

> The poor soul sat sighing by a sycamore tree,
>   Sing all a green willow.
> Her hand on her bosom, her head on her knee,
>   Sing willow, willow, willow.
> The fresh streams ran by her and murmured her moans,
>   Sing willow, willow, willow. (4.3.38–43)

Figure 2.1 *Hamlet and the players*. Drawing by Henry Stacy Marks (1851). Courtesy of the Folger Shakespeare Library.

Likely, this textual change reflects practical changes in playhouse personnel. The company 'did not always have a good singing boy to perform major female roles', and so the part of Desdemona (as well as a significant moment in the play) needed to be revised accordingly.[16] Something similar is probably at work in *Twelfth Night*. The opening scene seems to suggest a Viola who 'can sing' and converse with Orsino 'in many sorts of music' (1.2.53, 54). However, in the rest of the playtext as we have it, all of the songs are given to Feste instead, perhaps because the boy actor playing Viola's voice had broken.[17] In these kinds of textual alterations, we can glimpse some of the complex ways in which shared playhouse experiences, working environments, and practical realities shaped the texts of Shakespeare's plays we read today.

Shakespeare as Working Writer

Shakespeare's work as a writer, as we have seen, was directly influenced by his own experiences as an actor and his longstanding collaboration with the Lord Chamberlain's/King's Men across his career. But what about the more traditionally 'writerly' aspects of Shakespeare's dramaturgy? In what ways was his craft inflected by his education, his reading, and his creative engagement with his source materials? This section explores these questions to help round out our understanding of Shakespeare as a working playwright. And a useful place to begin is with the word 'playwright' itself. While we may be quick to define a playwright as simply one who writes plays, the etymology of the word suggests a more nuanced interpretation. The word 'wright' comes from the Old English word *wyrhta*, which meant an artificer or handicraftsman.[18] A playwright was thus like a cartwright (who crafts carts) or a wainwright (who build wagons) or a boatwright (who, not surprisingly, builds boats). Plays are *wrought*; they are 'designed, molded, fabricated, formed, contorted, sharpened, bent, formed, polished'.[19] As such, the word 'playwright' invokes not so much the 'lofty inspiration of the muses', but instead 'artisanal labour and manufacture of new commodities out of raw materials'.[20]

Like many English playwrights of the late sixteenth and early seventeenth centuries, Shakespeare came from the middle ranks of society and was raised in an artisanal household.[21] As the son of a glover, Shakespeare would have been familiar with the daily work of handicraft trades, and so the gap between Shakespeare's own work as a play*wright* and the manual labour of early modern craftspeople is not as great as it might initially seem. M. C. Bradbrook, whose early research on Shakespeare and work has been very influential to subsequent scholarship, explicitly discusses the work of the early modern playwright in terms of craft. As she writes:

The craftsman's 'form' is learnt in the process of making, by innumerable examples, not by recipe and precept. He works like a good cook. 'Take of fennel and cast in enough' say those maddening cookery books of Shakespeare's time. Familiarity and habituation; the long maturing of a seven years' apprenticeship made a craftsman.

The craft of making poetry and of making plays had long been familiar to Englishmen. It was a 'gentle' craft—like woodcraft or working fine metals.[22]

Bradbrook describes craftsmanship as a developmental process, one in which the maker/author is engaged in the study of exemplars and repeated observation of skills, patterns, and routines. It is fundamentally a communal process: it requires the work's creator to have a good understanding of the work's audience, use, and likely reception. As Bradbrook puts it: 'To look at a beautiful old piece of craftsmanship you need to know just for what sort of people it was designed, and how they were to use it.'[23] As we saw in the previous section, Shakespeare's deep understanding of the theatrical companies and audiences for which he wrote shaped his craft in numerous ways. Theatrical 'familiarity and habituation' helped Shakespeare's development as a working writer.

Shakespeare the playwright also learned his craft via his formal education in grammar school. After learning to read in an elementary or 'petty' school in Stratford-upon-Avon, Shakespeare would have moved on to the grammar school, where he would have been immersed in a highly rigorous programme of study. Students remained in grammar school for about ten or eleven years, during which time they would spend six days a week attending school from dawn until dusk. What would this grammar school education have been like? Students would have been introduced to the classics, and they would have received extensive training in both Latin and English grammar and in rhetoric. Shakespeare and his classmates would have spent their time 'reading, translating, and writing Latin, composing poems, essays, and arguments'.[24] They also learned to interpret Greek and Roman authors as models for both artistic and personal development. It was in the grammar school that Shakespeare would have likely first encountered the works of Ovid, Plutarch, Cicero, Virgil, and Seneca. Much of the day-to-day work consisted of memorization, repetition, and critical interpretation. But reading was always an active process in Shakespeare's grammar school (as it was in early modern culture more broadly); students were encouraged to engage in an ongoing dialogue with the texts they read, by adding marginal notations, reading aloud, and by identifying and evaluating texts for their rhetorical arguments.[25]

Several specific pedagogical methods from Shakespeare's grammar school education would have had a direct and long-lasting impact on his work as a playwright. To begin with, the practice of studying the classics would have been a highly embodied and even theatrical one for Shakespeare and his classmates. Oratorial training was a key component of grammar school education. Schoolboys were expected to learn to recite Latin prose and verse aloud, to debate formal questions in Latin, and to develop the 'proper pronunciation, clarity of enunciation, vocal emphasis and control, respect for rhythm and pitch, and the accompanying "action" of facial expression and bodily stance and gesture'.[26] In addition to memorized recitations, grammar school oratorical exercises also would have included in-class performances of scenes from classical drama. Such training emphasized the student's ability to impersonate a character in a lively way that fully embodied that character's persona and emotions. This process involved not just rhetorical skill, but also meticulous attention to gesture, voice, and facial expression. It should be no surprise, then, that the grammar school provided an excellent foundation for future actors and dramatists like Shakespeare. As Lynn Enterline has demonstrated, the 'embodied, performative aspects of training in Latin grammar and rhetoric' were a kind of 'daily theater' in their own right. They also played a significant role in the development of commercial theatre and theatrical practice in early modern England.[27]

Learning the classics was also done primarily through repeated exercises in translation. As a daily part of their classroom exercises, schoolboys were asked to translate passages of classical texts from Latin into English, and then back again into Latin. Then, students were instructed to compare the original source with their newly translated text. This process was known as 'bilingual' or double translation. In addition to being a challenging exercise, the work of double translation also encourages an intimate relationship between an author (or translator) and their source material. As Scott Newstok describes it: 'The effort makes you attend to the texture of texts; appreciate nuance; and close the distance across cultures and time. Ultimately, *translation is your way of learning your own language.*'[28] Like rhetorical and oratorical training, translation was an active process of exchange and intellectual development. Students had to know what their source material said, but they also had to know *how* the text worked structurally and artistically. And they had to make it their own. So, although today we might often think about translation as less 'original' than other forms of authorship, that was not a presumption made by early modern writers. Translation was a key part of how Shakespeare would have 'learned his own language' on his route to becoming a playwright.

Like translation, the act of imitation often gets a bad rap today. Imitation is typically understood as an explicitly derivative process, one dependent on (and subordinate to) an original source. In terms of the writing process, to describe something as an 'imitation' might seem like a pejorative dismissal of the writing's quality or even evoke concerns about plagiarism. Our current-day concept of plagiarism would have been unknown to Shakespeare, as modern copyright law did not exist until 1710. But more importantly, imitation, like translation, was central to the early modern grammar school education, and it was not a process of mere repetition or copying, but an embodied, active process of engaging intellectually with one's literary predecessors. Humanist pedagogy, as Janet Clare writes, 'was based on the selection of a model, and the replication of its argument and rhetorical strategies'.[29] Imitation was thus a lauded component of literary and linguistic training and, when done skilfully, it was considered to be essential to the art of literary creation. Indeed, the skill of imitation was often alluded to in the metaphors used to describe the process of writing in Shakespeare's England. One popular metaphor for the writing process, itself borrowed by Ben Jonson from Seneca, likened the author to a bee who selected from the 'choicest flowers' and turned their nectar into honey.[30] Imitation was an art, but it was also work: a process that involved skill and finesse.

For Shakespeare, then, writing always involved some form of rewriting. Beyond his grammar school training, his direct involvement with commercial theatre meant that he was well attuned to the demand for new material that built upon popular storylines and motifs from classical and contemporary drama. Early modern theatregoers' 'appetite for new plays' required Shakespeare to transform the dramatic narratives, characters, and themes of others to his own purposes and to suit new audiences. Following the humanist model of imitation and adaptation, nearly all of Shakespeare's plays 'revise or adapt a major source, as well as incorporating allusions or more local borrowings from a range of texts, including previous works by Shakespeare'.[31] Indeed, in a theatrical context, revisions were often heralded as a selling point, as they signalled that a play needed to be changed in order for it to remain current and draw audiences.[32] Playwrighting for Shakespeare thus involved an ongoing process of reading, writing, and rewriting to suit a changing theatrical and commercial landscape as well as shifts in audiences' tastes. Like the early modern theatrical world itself, this was a communal environment, not an isolated expression of creative genius. Shakespeare's 'practice as a playwright', as Gary Taylor notes, 'belonged to the social world of the artisan and the workshop, a world of collaborative trial-and-error tinkering'.[33] Shakespeare's distinctive skill lay in his ability to blend these various sources in creative and compelling ways to appeal to new Elizabethan and Jacobean audiences across a range of dramatic genres.

When Shakespeare actually sat down to write, the process was thus not entirely a solitary one, but an active process of reading, note-taking, and creative reimagining. In many ways this is not so different from many of our modern writing practices, if we stop to think about it. As I write this now, I am sitting at my desk surrounded by books that serve as references, sources, and general guides, and I construct my own written observations in an active (if unvocalized) dialogue with other scholars and prior studies. Similarly, Shakespeare's reading may have begun in the grammar school, but it continued throughout his working life as a writer and it provided him with rich resources from which he could draw throughout his career as a dramatist. Shakespeare read widely, and he frequently drew from a broad range of disparate sources when crafting his own plays. As Robert Miola has demonstrated, Shakespeare 'conjoins separate texts and traditions freely and unpredictably'. In *A Midsummer Night's Dream*, for instance, he borrows from ancient sources (including Ovid and Plutarch), medieval ones (notably Chaucer), and contemporary ones (such as the writings of Reginald Scot and Thomas Nashe).[34] It's likely that, as he wrote, Shakespeare would have had books nearby him as references and guides (in addition to others that he may have had stored in his memory). One of these books would have probably been what was known in the period as a 'commonplace' or 'table' book. These were texts in which authors copied passages from other works and added additional notes, a process of ongoing observation as well as a way to record ideas and quotations for future use. Shakespeare's 'reading' was thus not simply a set of texts, but a process:[35] it was an active and ongoing part of the work that constituted Shakespeare's life as a playwright.

Shakespeare's work as a playwright encompassed a broad range of theatrical and literary engagements. He was very much a man of the theatre, and he wrote his plays with the artistic and practical realities of his theatrical companies in mind. In addition, he worked intertextually with dramatic sources (classical and contemporary) as well as materials from a range of poetic and prose genres. None of this work was solitary, nor were the literary and theatrical components of his writing process easily separable from each other. What emerges from the evidence instead is an image of an active, collaborative artist whose works could not have been produced without the collective labours and energies of multiple people, both living and dead. To underscore that point, I want to conclude this discussion of Shakespeare as a working writer by briefly considering the work of the print shop that enabled Shakespeare's plays to circulate *as texts* in the world.

For most books today (including the one you are holding in your hand or reading on your e-reader), authors compose their text on a computer, and things like deletions, revisions, and even printing can be accomplished with a few keystrokes or the click of a mouse. Because much of the physical labour of book production has been significantly diminished by the advancement of printing technologies, we may be less likely to take account of the vast amount of work that went into printing books in Shakespeare's England. But after an author such as Shakespeare completed a manuscript, significant additional labour was required to bring that text to print. This work was done by workers in a print shop rather than the author, but it was nevertheless an essential component of how early modern literary works came to be. In the print shop, a worker known as a compositor would first need to decipher the handwriting of the manuscript. Then, the compositor would take individual letters of type from their storage cases and (by means of a handheld device called a composing stick) use them to recreate the words from the manuscript letter by letter. Each composing stick held about three lines of type, so this was a slow and laborious process. Once the stick was full, 'the compositor emptied it, placing the lines on a *galley*—a flat wooden board with a handle, like a paddle—until he had completed a page'.[36] It's worth noting as well that most compositors were 'encouraged to improve the punctuation and spelling' of the text they were working with,[37] so the process was just as textual and intellectual as it was mechanical. Once enough pages were completed to constitute a unit known as a *forme*, the compositor locked them into an iron chase. Then another worker, known as a pressman, would apply ink to the letters and press wet paper down upon them to create an impression. A corrector would then read over the printed sheets as they came off the press to spot errors and correct them on a rolling basis (although usually without discarding the earlier, faulty sheets). Each stage in this process required a great deal of time, care, and technical skill.[38]

This brief overview provides only a cursory glimpse at the labour that went into printing Shakespeare's plays. But it reminds us that the work of playwrighting with which Shakespeare was engaged neither started nor ended with him. Just as it would be misleading to draw any clear distinction between Shakespeare's writerly process and his work in and for the theatre, so too would it be a mistake to establish a strict division between the theatre, the authorial writing process, and the work of the print shop.[39] The work of creating, writing, and printing one of Shakespeare's plays was multifaceted and collaborative, and the evidence we have clearly suggests that work and art were not understood as opposing concepts by either Shakespeare or his contemporaries. That makes it somewhat surprising, then, that some of the earliest commentators on Shakespeare often *did* try to separate his artistic creations from the world of work. As we will see in the next section, however, those early assessments did not go unchallenged. An analysis of these early assessments reveals just how important Shakespeare's status as a working writer has historically been to evaluations of his plays, and how our own understanding of Shakespeare's work as a playwright can help us better understand his texts going forward.

Shakespeare, Work, and Early Commentators

How was Shakespeare's work as a writer understood by his earliest commentators? Did they distinguish between the labour of his writing and his creative artistry, or did they view Shakespeare's playwrighting as simultaneously both work and art? The answer to these questions is complex, as it depends in large part on conflicting ideas about authorship, creativity, and the value of work, ideas that differed from writer to writer and changed over time. But a brief exploration of these issues—and of the different viewpoints expressed by seventeenth- and eighteenth-century commentators—can help us see just how central concepts of work were to understanding and appreciating Shakespeare's artistry, even when work was depicted as an antithesis of creative endeavour. We can begin with perhaps one of the most famous (and earliest) descriptions of Shakespeare-as-playwright, the preface to the 1623 First Folio addressed to the 'Great Variety of Readers', and written by the volume's compilers, John Heminge and Henry Condell. In that preface, they praise Shakespeare as a 'happy imitator of Nature', and describe his writing process as an effortless one: 'His mind and hand went together: and what he thought, he uttered with that easiness, that we have scarce received from him a blot in his papers.'[40] In their, admittedly idealized, vision, Shakespeare's plays come to him easily—so easily, in fact, that he almost never needs to strike out an individual word or revise in any way! Of course, we know now that Shakespeare certainly did revise, and it's more than likely that Heminge and Condell were themselves deliberately exaggerating the 'ease' of Shakespeare's writing process. Still, this image, prominently placed at the beginning of the First Folio, sets up an apparent contrast between Shakespeare's dramatic output and any type of hard effort or labour.

This distinction would be drawn more clearly in the later seventeenth and eighteenth centuries. As Jonathan Bate notes, the prevailing image of Shakespeare in the eighteenth century was that he was a 'natural genius, the great poet of imagination'.[41] This was an idea that came to prominence in the second half of the seventeenth century. For John Milton, Shakespeare eschewed 'slow-endeavoring art' in favour of 'easy numbers'.[42] For John Dryden, Shakespeare's natural talent was far more important than his learning:

> All the Images of Nature were still present to him, and he drew them not laboriously, but luckily: when he describes any thing, you more than see it, you feel it too. Those who accuse him to have wanted learning, give him the greater commendation: he was naturally learn'd; he needed not the spectacles of Books to read Nature; he look'd inwards, and found her there.[43]

Of course, we know now that this assessment is a false one: Shakespeare was an avid reader and adaptor of a wide range of prose, poetic, and dramatic materials. But the idea of Shakespeare as a natural talent rather than a hardworking, learned artist was frequently articulated in the writings of early English commentators, especially in the eighteenth century. Often these characterizations were overtly critical in tone, disparaging Shakespeare for his seeming lack of learning or his apparent rejection of the formal rules of classical drama in many of his plays. But in addition to their function as aesthetic critiques, they also served to dissociate Shakespeare's artistry from serious effort or labour.

We can see this tension between artistry and work quite clearly in the eighteenth-century commentary of Samuel Johnson. In his *Preface* of 1765, Johnson reflects at length on Shakespeare's artistic legacy and on the qualities that distinguish him as a playwright. Johnson is arguably one of the earliest critics to associate Shakespeare clearly (and in a sustained fashion) with what we might think of as the everyday. Writing about what he calls 'vernacular criticism'—an approach to literary works that is 'at home with, or indigenous to a contemporary idiom of assumptions and presuppositions about how to account for the actions of ordinary people'—Michael Bristol singles out Johnson's *Preface* as the 'most fully codified' of such 'vernacular' approaches in the eighteenth century.[44] Much like Dryden, Johnson considered Shakespeare to be the 'poet of nature', but what is distinctive about Johnson's assessment is his assertion that Shakespeare's 'natural' inclinations are of a piece with the 'practical axioms and domestick wisdom' that filled his plays. As an artist, Shakespeare 'caught his ideas from the living world'.[45] As Bristol notes, however, the everyday-ness of Shakespeare was problematic for Johnson, who recognized the vernacular appeal of Shakespeare's language, but emphatically did not share the moral values it represented. So, although Johnson acknowledges that Shakespeare's 'domestick wisdom' is the root of much of his artistic worth, he simultaneously criticizes him for creating vulgar ideas and characters. Shakespeare, according to Johnson, was writing for a 'rude people', and he asserts: 'Those to whom our authour's labours were exhibited had more skill in pomps or processions than in poetical language, and perhaps wanted some visible and discriminated events, as comments on the dialogue.'[46] Johnson's praise of Shakespeare's natural and domestic talent founders when it encounters the material realities of Shakespeare's theatre. Johnson approves of Shakespeare's engagement with the 'living world', in other words, up to the point where that world becomes populated by actual 'rude' people and bodies.

In this dismissal of Shakespeare's audiences as a spectacle-loving multitude, Johnson flirts with the idea of Shakespeare himself as a working writer who displays his labour in the theatre. However, the concept of labour enters the discussion here in a primarily pejorative sense: Shakespeare gaudily exhibits his labours to the undiscriminating multitudes of theatregoers. When Johnson hints at the idea of Shakespeare as a worker elsewhere in the *Preface*, the image is again a negative one. Johnson criticizes Shakespeare, for instance, for neglecting the ending to his plays: 'When he found himself near the end of his work, and in view of his reward, he shortened the labour, to snatch the profit.'[47] Johnson here conjures up the image of Shakespeare as a bad or lazy worker, one who cuts out early on the job in order to claim a quick financial reward. The concept of work thus enters Johnson's critique of Shakespeare's authorship as an explicitly negative construction, an unfortunate blemish on Shakespeare's artistic processes. The whiff of commercialism—the very notion that Shakespeare might have been interested in earning profits from his plays—further colours Johnson's assessment of Shakespeare's literary value.

Johnson's invocations of Shakespeare as a labourer—as disparaging as they are—are fairly isolated moments in the *Preface*. More typical of Johnson's account is the assertion that Shakespeare is in fact not a worker, a status that makes him all the more praiseworthy as an artist. Johnson, for instance, argues that Shakespeare excels at comedy (including the comic scenes within tragedies) producing in the process 'without labour, what no labour can improve'. 'His tragedy', Johnson writes, 'seems to be skill, his comedy to be instinct.'[48] Johnson commends Shakespeare for producing drama that is divorced from, rather than dependent on, authorial work as such. On this point, Johnson distinguishes what he characterizes as the 'work of a correct and regular writer' from Shakespeare's processes of composition. The first, Johnson argues, operates like a 'garden accurately formed and diligently planted'. Shakespeare's plays (and his process of play-making), on the other hand, resemble 'a forest, in which oaks extend their branches, and pines tower in the air' and which is 'interspersed sometimes with weeds and brambles'.[49] Johnson associates the precision of a 'correct and regular writer' with the work of human cultivation, the diligent labour required to produce and maintain an 'accurately formed' garden, likely a reference to the highly stylized and developed English landscape gardens that were popular in the eighteenth century. Through this image, work gets defined in opposition to both nature and leisure; the business of cultivation stands against the almost wayward, natural growth of the unruly forest of Shakespeare's artistry.

Johnson, then, defines Shakespearian authorship as the opposite of labour, yet he also acknowledges at times the 'everyday' qualities of Shakespeare's writing. Within the pages of the *Preface*, we can thus trace a tension between 'elite' artistry and 'everyday' work in the evaluation of Shakespeare's literary output, a tension that Johnson himself never completely resolves (and one that we'll return to in the Epilogue to this book). But the tradition of valuing Shakespeare because he did *not* work (as a writer) did not go unopposed by early commentators. Indeed, we can return all the way back to the 1623 First Folio to glimpse another perspective on Shakespeare's artistry as it relates to work. Here we find Ben Jonson's famous commendatory poem on Shakespeare, 'To the Memory of My Beloved, The Author, Master William Shakespeare, And What He Hath Left Us'. Jonson praises the naturalness of Shakespeare's verse, but he also draws attention to the skill embedded within it. Jonson writes that Shakespeare's lines 'were so richly spun and woven so fit' that it made Nature proud. Using imagery from weaving and textile production, Jonson insists that Shakespeare's 'natural' poetic artistry is directly related to his craft. A few lines later in the poem, Jonson extends this idea further:

Yet must I not give nature all: thy art,
My gentle Shakespeare, must enjoy a part.
For though the poet's matter nature be,
His art doth give the fashion. And, that he
Who casts to write a living line must sweat
(Such as thine are) and strike the second heat
Upon the muses' anvil; turn the same,
(And himself with it) that he thinks to frame;
Or for the laurel he may gain a scorn,
For a good poet's made as well as born. (55–64)[50]

Here Jonson turns to the workaday image of the blacksmith's forge to describe (and laud) Shakespeare's work as a playwright. The image of the poet hammering away at the 'muses' anvil' in a repeated attempt to 'turn' and 'frame' his verses emphasizes the hard, physical labour that writing entails. Shakespeare's artistry, in other words, is a direct product of his hard (even sweaty!) work.

This image of the labouring writer is one that Jonson returns to frequently in his own writing; he often uses metaphors of labour to describe 'the writing process of the ideal poet and good man'.[51] In some ways, Jonson was an outlier among poets of his time. Literary authorship, after all, had long been associated with leisure and ease, as when Sir Philip Sidney referred to his extensive prose romance, the *Arcadia*, as 'this idle work of mine'.[52] But those ideas, as we saw in Chapter 1, were gradually beginning to change in Shakespeare's lifetime, and this was especially true where the theatre was concerned. In his verses in the First Folio, Jonson offers a contrasting view that emphasizes the physical effort that is intrinsic to good writing. Jonson's Shakespeare is both gentle and a sweating labourer, a picture of poetic authority that contrasts sharply with Heminge and Condell's praise of Shakespeare as one who wrote 'with that easiness, that we have scarce received from him a blot in his papers'. It is in Jonson's lines that we can see Shakespeare the craftsman, the playwright for whom work and art were of a piece. And despite the contrasting views that would be espoused by critics in subsequent decades, it is Jonson's early perspective that accords most with what we know today about Shakespeare's work as an actor, theatrical professional, reader, writer, and reviser. Following Jonson's lead, we can bring this understanding of Shakespeare as a working artist with us as we turn to his plays and examine them in more detail. As we will explore over the next four chapters, Shakespeare's dramatic output, like the playwright himself, disrupts any clear division between work and art. Instead, as we'll see, work remains a vital component of Shakespeare's plays throughout his career, affecting his characters, plots, themes, and language in rich and sometimes surprising ways.

Shakespeare and Work. Michelle M. Dowd, Oxford University Press. © Michelle M. Dowd 2026.
DOI: 10.1093/9780191998096.003.0003

3

Service and Domestic Work

Now that we have a better understanding of Shakespeare's world of work and how he participated in the labour economy as an actor, writer, and theatrical professional, we can turn to his plays in more detail to consider how they represent several distinct kinds of labour. We start in this chapter with one of the most ubiquitous forms of work in Shakespeare's England and one of the most frequently represented in his plays: service, especially domestic service. Shakespeare includes servant characters in nearly all of his plays, and in the vast majority of them servants participate significantly in the dialogue and dramatic action.[1] Service as a form of work was undergoing a significant transformation during Shakespeare's lifetime, as we'll see, which made servants and the broader concept of 'service' a particularly rich topic for theatrical representation in the period. This chapter offers an overview of the role of service and domestic work in Shakespeare's plays, and it demonstrates the vital importance of servants and their labour to Shakespearian characterization, dialogue, action, and dramatic structure. Following an introductory discussion of early modern service and domestic work, we will explore how Shakespeare stages service in plays such as *King Lear*, *Othello*, and *Antony and Cleopatra*. The next section of the chapter will take a closer look at women's service and domestic work. Focusing on *Twelfth Night*, this section demonstrates how Shakespeare shaped the plot of this great comedy around women's domestic labour and their evolving economic roles in the period. The chapter concludes with a discussion of service as it relates to global practices of racialized slavery. Looking at *The Tempest* in particular, we can gain a fuller understanding of how Shakespeare's staged representations of service were influenced by ideas about race and bondage.

Service in Shakespeare's England: Definitions and Contexts

What did it mean to be a servant in Shakespeare's time? Although the concept of the service economy may be very familiar to us today, we are less accustomed to (and generally less comfortable with) thinking about individuals as servants. If asked to conjure up an image of a domestic servant, we might hark back to popular media representations that depict nineteenth- and early twentieth-century settings, such as the popular television series *Downton Abbey*, which depicts the lives of an aristocratic family and their household of servants in the post-Edwardian era. But although these kinds of 'upstairs/downstairs' representations of masters and servants suggest clearly drawn class boundaries, the reality of service was often quite different. This was especially true in Shakespeare's England, as the meaning of 'service' in the sixteenth and early seventeenth centuries was much more fluid and complex than a simple dichotomy (master/servant) could convey.

Like the category of work itself, service is a term that resists easy definition. In the broadest use of the term during Shakespeare's lifetime, everyone could be understood as 'in service' to someone else according to the prevailing hierarchical models of social order. So, for instance, members of the nobility were servants of the king or queen, and even kings and queens were servants of God. Taken in this broad sense, service 'transcended class barriers' and encompassed all of early modern society.[2] The language associated with service was equally flexible in the period. The word 'service', for instance, could signify the performance of specific household tasks, but it could also refer to courtly love, religious ritual, and military conduct, to name just a few of the many possibilities. Given this wide range of meanings, it can be helpful to distinguish between two primary concepts of service in the period: occupational service and hierarchical service. As David Schalkwyk defines these concepts, occupational service is primarily an economic condition connected with employment, usually for a temporary period of time. It included multiple forms of domestic service as well as apprenticeship (which we will consider more fully in the next chapter). Hierarchical service was a broader, political concept that formed the basis of early modern England's stratified social order.[3] In this chapter, our primary focus will be on the first category—occupational service—and specifically the work of household servants, the form of service that Shakespeare represents most frequently in his plays.[4]

Service and domestic work are a vital part of Shakespeare's dramatic world. In many of the plays, service provides an important backdrop to the main action, offering us a glimpse of the household life of Shakespeare's fictional families and establishing key details of mood and setting. In *Romeo and Juliet*, for instance, servants set the stage for arguably the most momentous scene in the entire play: the party at the Capulet house, where the two star-crossed lovers meet for the first time. The scene opens with Peter and several other 'servingmen' who enter 'with napkins', a signal that they are preparing the house for guests and an elaborate meal. Their dialogue captures the energy and spirit of frantic preparation that prepares the audience for the crucial meeting to come:

> [PETER] Where's Potpan, that he helps not to take away? He shift a trencher, he scrape a trencher!
> FIRST SERVINGMAN When good manners shall lie all in one or two men's hands, and they unwashed too, 'tis a foul thing.
> [PETER] Away with the joint-stools, remove the court-cupboard, look to the plate. Good thou, save me a piece of marzipan, and, as thou loves me, let the porter let in Susan Grindstone and Nell. Anthony and Potpan!
> SECOND SERVINGMAN Ay, boy, ready.
> [PETER] You are looked for and called for, asked for and sought for, in the great chamber.
> [FIRST] SERVINGMAN We cannot be here and there too. Cheerly, boys! Be brisk a while, and the longest liver take all. (1.5.1–15)

The lively conversation between these domestic servants draws its vitality from offhand references to the details of household labour, especially in this case the work involved in food preparation and hosting. Potpan (probably the name of a kitchen servant) is chastised for not attending to the wooden plates ('trenchers') in a timely fashion, while the onstage servants are enjoined to move the 'joint-stools' (likely meant for seating at the banquet), relocate the sideboard (the 'court-cupboard'), and secure and position the silverware (the 'plate').

And though the short exchange is staged as a friendly, even jolly instance of domestic business, the servingman's rather sardonic comment that '[w]e cannot be here and there too' highlights both the urgency of the moment and the sheer volume of work required to ensure that the Capulets' party is a success.

Similar moments occur throughout the Shakespearian canon. Often these moments are fleeting, yet they enable Shakespeare to suggest the richness and complexity of the various households he depicts. In *The Merchant of Venice*, for instance, Lorenzo and Lancelot discuss dinner preparations in Portia's house and allude to the offstage work of household servants. As Lorenzo instructs Lancelot: 'Go to thy fellows; bid them cover the table, serve in the meat, and we will come in to dinner' (3.5.53–5). Brief comments such as this one help establish setting and tone, in this case attesting to the liveliness and economic productivity of Portia's household. In other cases, as we saw with *Romeo and Juliet*, the work of domestic service becomes more visible on stage. In *Coriolanus*, for example, servants once again set the scene for a crucial meeting, this time between Coriolanus and his sworn enemy Aufidius. When Coriolanus arrives at Aufidius' home and offers to join forces with him, he is initially stopped and questioned by several servingmen who are in the middle of preparing for a feast. In the scene's opening lines, the First Servingman berates his fellows for their delays in bringing food and drink to the table: 'Wine, wine, wine! What service is here? I think our fellows are asleep' (4.5.1–2). As in *Romeo and Juliet*, the onstage banter between the servants conveys the frenetic energy of domestic hospitality, underscoring its significance to household order and general reputation. In this instance, the servants also provide an onstage 'audience' for the pivotal meeting between Aufidius and Coriolanus, offering extensive commentary on the exchange once the two military leaders have departed the stage. These examples suggest just how ubiquitous domestic service is in Shakespeare's plays, where it often constitutes a key part of his dramatic contexts and settings. But the function of service and domestic work in Shakespeare is more varied and complex than these quick examples might suggest. To understand more fully how service work shapes the fabric of Shakespeare's plays, we first need to consider how service was changing in the period and why it was such a hotly debated category of work.

At the turn of the seventeenth century in England, the institution of service was in the process of changing from a feudal model based primarily on loyalty and obligation to a wage labour system focused on protecting property rights. Under the feudal ideal of 'universal service', labourers offered their services to masters and mistresses in return for protection, and they might remain with the same household for many years. This feudal model dominated medieval society, and it continued to hold sway throughout much of the early modern period as well. But by the end of the sixteenth century, this understanding of service was slowly giving way to a system in which servants negotiated yearly contracts for wages with employers. Servants in this period were typically young people who had left home to enter into service, and they usually changed masters frequently (often annually), moving from place to place until they married and formed a household of their own (in the ideal scenario). Servants worked in both rural and urban settings throughout England, and they constituted an extremely large part of the workforce: according to one estimate, 'perhaps 60 per cent of the English population aged between fifteen and twenty-four lived as servants' in the households of those who needed their labour.[5]

The causes of these shifts in the service economy were complex, but one significant development was the change in the structure and formation of elite English households. Between 1590 and 1620, for instance, the size of aristocratic households was sharply reduced—'from an average of one hundred or so each to three or four dozen'—resulting in the replacement of long-term domestic servants with 'short-term hirings on a cash basis'.[6] As a result, as Michael Neill has argued, 'the notion of what it meant to be a "servant" was progressively narrowed and specialized until it came to refer almost exclusively to a form of domestic wage-labor, a potentially degrading occupation fundamentally distinct from other forms of "service"'.[7] Such changes were neither uniform nor linear, and contradictory viewpoints about the nature of service helped spur dialogue and debate on the topic well into the seventeenth century. Indeed, we see these historical changes reflected in the theatrical world of which Shakespeare was such a vital part. Members of early modern playing companies were officially servants to their noble or aristocratic patrons (hence the names of many of the period's theatrical companies, such as the 'Lord Admiral's Men' and the 'Lord Chamberlain's Men'). At the same time, as we saw in

Chapter 1, the players were 'increasingly beholden' to the economic demands of the commercial theatre and, as such, they 'belonged more to the fluid world of urban commerce than to the ostensibly unchanging domain of feudal retainers'.[8] Early modern players were thus positioned often uneasily between older and new forms of service. Given this theatrical context, it is not surprising that Shakespeare drew inspiration from the 'tense coexistence' of 'fiercely conflicting attitudes' about service and turned it into a rich topic of exploration in his plays.[9]

The fundamental transformation of the service economy from one based (at least in theory) on principles of hospitality and loyalty to one based primarily on economic motives and the need for a temporary workforce is neatly summarized by Orlando's response to his old servant Adam in *As You Like It*, written in 1599:

> O good old man, how well in thee appears
> The constant service of the antique world,
> When service sweat for duty, not for meed!
> Thou art not for the fashion of these times,
> Where none will sweat but for promotion,
> And having that do choke their service up
> Even with the having. It is not so with thee. (2.3.57–63)

In Orlando's wistful commentary, 'meed' and 'promotion' have replaced 'constant service' and 'duty' as the primary characteristics of dependent household labour. The 'fashion of these times' requires that domestic servants be motivated by money rather than by loyalty, a change that Orlando clearly laments. At the same time, his praise of Adam is a direct response to a monetary transaction: Adam has just given Orlando the 'five hundred crowns' (39) from his 'youthful wages' (68) that he has saved up over the years so that he can flee his childhood home and escape the wrath of his brother without resorting to begging or a 'thievish living' (34). Adam clearly epitomizes the more traditional, feudal model of service from 'the antique world', but at the same time the generous assistance he provides to Orlando is firmly based in a more modern economy of wages and thrifty savings; he is both the idealized, faithful servant and one who fully understands the monetary details of domestic work. Adam's position thus draws attention to some of the significant socio-economic changes that were transforming service during Shakespeare's lifetime. What Shakespeare does so well in *As You Like It* and throughout his oeuvre is to rework and reimagine these historical shifts so that they become central to his plots and characters and deeply imbricated in the thematic and creative worlds of his plays writ large. It is Adam, after all, who enables Orlando's escape to Arden, the catalyst for the rest of the play's romantic action and a precursor to its ultimate familial resolutions. Just as Adam's service includes aspects of both older and newer models of domestic labour, so too does his pivotal function in this scene with Orlando look both backward to familial conflict and danger and ahead to novel forms of community and romantic attachment.

Staging Service

Shakespeare returns again and again to the changing landscape of the service economy as a rich resource for dramatic plotting, memorable characterizations, and the exploration of crucial themes, such as the nature of power, obedience, and social order. He is particularly fond of staging moments that throw into question the very nature of service work, and he asks his audiences to consider questions such as: what makes a good servant as opposed to a bad servant? What role should domestic servants play in a household, and what are the limits of that role? What responsibilities do servants owe to their masters and when, if ever, can they disobey them? In *As You Like It*, Adam's service is presented as relatively straightforward, in that it is characterized by his absolute fealty to Orlando and his willingness to provide him with financial support for his journey to Arden. But in other plays, domestic servants behave more unpredictably or wilfully, through acts of role playing, deception, disobedience, and even radical acts of loyalty. Shakespeare frequently stages these complexities to memorable effect.

The Taming of the Shrew offers a good example of an early play in which Shakespeare not only depicts several domestic servants across different households, but also showcases the increasing malleability of 'service' as a category of work in the period. When Petruchio takes Katherine to his country house following their wedding, we see that his household is filled with servants. Grumio (Petruchio's longstanding, much beleaguered servant) is informing another servant, Curtis, about their master's immanent arrival with his new bride. His questioning hints at the vast amount of work necessary to maintaining an elite country home, such as Petruchio's:

> Where's the cook? Is supper ready, the house trimmed, rushes strewed, cobwebs swept, the servingmen in their new fustian, the white stockings, and every officer his wedding garment on? Be the Jacks fair within, the Jills fair without, the carpets laid, and everything in order? (4.1.40–5)

As in *Coriolanus* and *Romeo and Juliet*, this quickfire list of questions itemizes household work and suggests frenzied behind-the-scenes preparations that (in this case) will only be amplified by Petruchio's own outlandish behaviour upon his arrival home. Indeed, the sheer number of servants (thirteen) who apparently staff this country estate signal its cultural importance, highlight Petruchio's wealth and social standing, and attest to the complex social world in which Katherine will soon find herself (and where she will be 'tamed' in part by being forced to demonstrate her proper management of both household goods and servants).[10] Grumio instructs Curtis:

> Call forth Nataniel, Joseph, Nicholas, Philip, Walter, Sugarsop, and the rest. Let their heads be sleekly combed, their blue coats brushed, and their garters of an indifferent knit. Let them curtsy with their left legs and not presume to touch a hair of my master's horse-tail till they kiss their hands. Are they all ready? (4.1.79–84)

Grumio's invocation of these numerous household servants helps build up the dramatic tension prior to Petruchio's and Katherine's arrival. It also highlights his attempt to assert domestic order by insisting upon the neat and carefully presented 'blue coat' uniforms, traditional to servants in the period, and the displays of deference implied by the request to 'curtsy'. In part, this scene helps set the stage for the extended emphasis on domestic order that will follow in Petruchio's 'taming' of Katherine. But it also attests to the profound disorder that exists at the centre of this household, a disorder that must be resolved (perhaps incompletely, depending on how we read the play's ending) in order to restore domestic and marital harmony.

Shakespeare's representation of male domestic servants in *The Taming of the Shrew* is indebted to classical models, such as the comedies of Plautus and Terence, which prominently feature servant characters. Many of these characters take on certain 'stock' roles as, for instance 'stolid blockheads who serve mostly as whipping posts', and, more commonly, trickster figures who scheme to assist their (usually young) masters.[11] Grumio is one version of the first type, although Shakespeare develops his character beyond that of the abused servant to showcase his loyalty to Petruchio, his sparks of verbal wit, and his independent scheming. In the figure of Tranio, however, Shakespeare takes the classical model of the wily servant and makes it a centrepiece of the play's subplot. For most of the play, Tranio disguises himself as his master, Lucentio, in order to pose as a suitor to Baptista's younger daughter, Bianca (Katherine's sister). The ruse enables Lucentio to win Bianca's love in private, in disguise as a tutor. And although the shifting of roles via disguise is put into play by Lucentio and fully sanctioned by him, Tranio's actions as Lucentio suggest that the roles of master and servant may not be as clearly distinguished as the traditional model of Elizabethan social order might have presupposed. Tranio, it must be said, does an excellent job of 'being' his master, Lucentio. In the scene where Baptista asks Tranio/Lucentio to vie for Bianca's hand against the elderly suitor Gremio by offering his daughter the 'greatest dower', Tranio not only holds his own, but also triumphs outright by confidently articulating the wealth he would bring to the marriage in forthright and assured terms:

> I am my father's heir and only son.
> If I may have your daughter to my wife
> I'll leave her houses three or four as good,
> Within rich Pisa walls, as any one
> Old Signor Gremio has in Padua,
> Besides two thousand ducats by the year
> Of fruitful land, all which shall be her jointure.
> What, have I pinched you, Signor Gremio? (2.1.360–7)

The audience has no way to verify whether Tranio's accounting is accurate or not. What matters here is his adept *performance* of mastery, his skill at role-playing, and his ability to effortlessly sound and act like a wealthy heir. It is through depictions such as this that we can see Shakespeare using the changing nature of service work in the period to his theatrical advantage. Taking the classical trickster servant model and adapting it to a late Elizabethan world where service was rapidly becoming both a more temporary form of work and one that did not necessarily designate a fixed social rank, Shakespeare often stages the male domestic servant as a figure caught in between older and newer models of service, one whose labour involves both subordination and independent creativity. In *The Taming of the Shrew*, Tranio performs a kind of disruptive service, in that he acts independently in many instances and plays a role well above his social station. However, Shakespeare tempers that disruption by casting Tranio as ultimately a loyal servant who only behaves as he does to help his master achieve his own version of domestic harmony, mirroring the movement towards traditional family ordering depicted in the play's main 'taming' plot. Servants in both plots thus help ensure comedic resolution, but their work must often be improvisatory, disorderly, or even socially subversive in order to reach those ends.

Shakespeare will go on to explore this idea that a good servant can (and, indeed, often must) be disobedient to his master in several of his late tragedies and romances. In these later plays, the friction between older and newer models of service is often not depicted in strictly economic terms. Instead, Shakespeare frequently transforms domestic service and its inherent tensions into a powerful vehicle for exploring such topics as political and personal loyalty, the limits of obedience, and the virtue of reasonable dissent. In *Antony and Cleopatra*, for example, Antony's faithful servant Eros ultimately chooses suicide over honouring his master's request to kill him. After his defeat in battle, Antony commands Eros to draw 'his honest sword' to kill him, reminding Eros that he had previously sworn to perform this duty as part of his service to Antony (4.15.79). 'Do it at once', Antony exclaims, 'Or thy precedent services are all | But accidents unpurposed' (82–4). But rather than doing 'that which all the Parthian darts, | Though enemy, lost aim and could not', Eros instead stabs himself and thus escapes 'the sorrow | Of Antony's death' (70–1, 94–5). Rather than depicting Eros as wrong to disobey Antony, Shakespeare instead encourages audiences to respond with sympathy, even admiration, for his action. When Antony praises Eros as '[t]hrice nobler than myself' following his suicide, he primes the audience to view his servant's disobedience as an honourable act of self-actualization.

Shakespeare returns to the question of justifiable disobedience in his profound meditations on the nature of love, loyalty, and obedience in *King Lear*. The play's opening scene immediately pushes these issues to the forefront by staging the contest between Lear's three daughters over which of them, in Lear's words, 'doth love us most' (Folio, 1.1.51). When Cordelia refuses to play the rhetorical game and succumb to public flattery of her father, she is promptly disinherited. The Earl of Kent, however, publicly takes her side and chastises Lear for his actions, for which he is banished. The noble Kent will soon disguise himself as the lowly Caius and return to Lear as his devoted servant. As he tells himself: 'If thou canst serve where thou dost stand condemned, | So may it come thy master, whom thou lov'st, | Shall find thee full of labours' (1.4.5–7). Shakespeare presents Kent as a voice of reason throughout the play, a servant who is willing to challenge his master when he finds him in the wrong. Unlike the obsequious Oswald, Goneril's steward, Kent 'displays his total commitment to the bond of service to his monarch precisely by *defying* him'.[12]

But the most shocking moment of servant disobedience in the tragedy (and arguably in all of Shakespeare) is the scene featuring the Duke of Cornwall's unnamed servant later in the play when he intervenes during the blinding of the Duke of Gloucester. Cornwall and his wife, Lear's daughter Regan, bind Gloucester to a chair, accusing him of treason because he has aided Lear. Cornwall proceeds to torture Gloucester, first putting out one of his eyes, and then turning to take the other (3.7.65–9). At that moment, the servant speaks:

> SERVANT Hold your hand, my lord.
> I have served you ever since I was a child,
> But better service have I never done you
> Than now to bid you hold.
> REGAN How now, you dog!
> SERVANT If you did wear a bear upon your chin
> I'd shake it on this quarrel. [*To Cornwall*] What do you mean?
> CORNWALL My villein!
> SERVANT Nay then, come on, and take the chance of anger.
> *They draw and fight* (3.7.70–7)

This is an extraordinary moment. Certainly, the violence of the scene is excessive and gruesome, forcing the audience to come to terms with the ugly extremes of political and familial conflict. But the scene is also notable for the audacity of the servant's actions. Indeed, Cornwall's servant isn't just disobeying orders (since none have explicitly been given to him); he is instead wilfully intervening and violently assaulting his master. Not surprisingly, such behaviour was usually viewed as a serious crime in the period. A servant who killed his master or mistress, for instance, was considered to have committed not just murder, but the more serious charge of petty treason. And yet, clearly Shakespeare has positioned his audience to side with the servant rather than with Cornwall, especially given the viciousness of the attack on Gloucester. As Richard Strier notes, 'Shakespeare is presenting the most radical possible sociopolitical act in a way that can only be interpreted as calling for his audience's approval.'[13] Even though the servant dies at Regan's hand, by drawing attention to his unprompted disobedience at this wrenching moment, Shakespeare transforms service into a central dramatic metaphor for political and social duty. By defining this act of defiance as 'better service', Shakespeare exposes the limitations of traditional models that prioritized the absolute loyalty of domestic servants and instead suggests the powerful force and even, at times, the necessity of more volatile acts of will.

Nowhere does Shakespeare explore these tensions between older and newer forms of service to greater effect than in *Othello*. In the figure of the duplicitous yet fiercely articulate Iago, Shakespeare presents us with what is arguably the most complex male servant figure in the entire canon. Iago is not a domestic servant in the traditional sense, but is instead Othello's ensign, his servant within the military hierarchy of the day. As Michael Neill explains, 'In the absence of a fully professional army organized by the state, military enlistment was necessarily thought of in quasi-feudal terms as a form of "service" founded on a mutual arrangement of duties and reward.'[14] Individuals thus served a captain or general (the commander of their company) and were bound to him as part of his entourage. In *Othello*, then, Iago and Cassio (Othello's lieutenant) are 'as much a part of the general's military 'household' as courtiers like Kent and Gloucester are members of the royal household in *Lear*'.[15] In the opening act of the tragedy, having been passed over for a promotion by Othello (who has given it to Cassio instead), Iago gives a long speech explicitly lamenting the 'curse of service' (1.1.34). He tells Roderigo that traditional relationships between masters and servants have been undermined, as older models of loyalty have been replaced by newer paradigms of patronage and personal influence (what he calls 'letter and affection') (35). His detailed tirade touches on many of the concerns raised by actual servants and other commentators in the period, many of whom critiqued the increased economic insecurity of newer service arrangements and pointed to a loss of mutual obligation between servants and masters. For instance, Iago explains to Roderigo:

> You shall mark
> Many a duteous and knee-crooking knave
> That, doting on his own obsequious bondage,
> Wears out his time much like his master's ass
> For naught but provender, and when he's old, cashiered. (44–8)

Iago complains about the lack of fair recompense for the 'duteous' servant who works diligently for his master yet earns 'naught by provender' (i.e. animal feed). In this assessment, service is not a mutual relationship, but merely an exploitative commercial contract. By pronouncing this sentiment in his very first appearance in the play, Iago may very well have provoked a good degree of audience sympathy, as such complaints about service were commonplace in the period.[16] And of course, Iago's ability to compel the allegiance of his audience is one of his trademark characteristics in this tragedy. But, in the true protean fashion that will mark his character throughout the play, Iago quickly shifts course to describe a different kind of servant: the duplicitous one who may be 'trimmed in forms and visages of duty', but '[k]eep yet their hearts attending on themselves' (50–1). They provide 'shows of service', while serving their own interests (lining 'their coats') (52–3). 'Such a one', Iago concludes, 'do I profess myself' (55). Here we see the disobedient yet crafty servant expressing his will with a tenacity and force that will set the entire play on its terrible path towards domestic tragedy.

In introducing Iago to his audience, Shakespeare draws on historical changes in the service economy to help shape Iago's complexities as a character, including his notoriously inscrutable motives. Why does Iago seek such revenge against Othello? Part of the answer seems tethered to his resentment of service and its 'obsequious bondage', a sentiment, again, that may have resonated with many in the audience. But at the same time, his eager embrace of the role of the deceptive servant who works only to serve his own interests enables him to carry out his elaborate plots against Othello. In doing so, Iago takes the mercenary aspects of the service economy to their most extreme and feared conclusion, ultimately leading to his master's death. As Iago memorably summarizes his position: 'I follow him to serve my turn upon him. | We cannot all be masters, nor all masters | Cannot be truly followed' (1.1.42–4). In Iago, we find a striking example of how Shakespeare uses service work to fundamentally shape characterization and plant the seeds for great drama. Shakespeare takes the realities of the early modern service economy, including the historical changes it was undergoing in the period, and transforms them into vivid theatre, staging crucial questions about loyalty, exploitation, and obedience in the process.

Women and Service in *Twelfth Night*

As we've seen, socio-economic changes in early modern England created a new kind of service economy, one that demanded an economically diverse and geographically mobile workforce that could be employed on a temporary basis. These changes were particularly significant for women, since domestic service was by far the most common occupation for adolescent Englishwomen in the period. Like men, women at all social levels participated in the service economy: poor families might hire a single maidservant to help with the kitchen, laundry, and aspects of household production, while aristocratic families would often take in the daughters of relatives or close connections to learn the skills of housewifery and deportment as they served members of the household.[17] The typical maidservant in Shakespeare's England would have been tasked with a wide variety of basic chores, including cooking, cleaning, doing laundry, serving food and drink, minding children, running errands, and other aspects of household management.[18] Many of these tasks were similar to those performed by male servants. However, women in service raised a distinctive set of social concerns, given their imprecisely defined status as single women who were no longer living in their birth homes, but were not yet wives. Given a sexual double standard that placed greater scrutiny on women's sexuality and demanded chastity in order to secure proper lineage and inheritance through heterosexual marriage, women in service were expected to follow a clear trajectory that led directly from service to marriage. In reality, however, that path was often far from straightforward, frequently due to a lack of financial resources.[19]

Shakespeare memorably explores women's service in *Twelfth Night*, a comedy that gains much of its energy from the action of two female servants and their path towards marriage. Women in service anchor both of *Twelfth Night*'s plots: the main plot by Viola (Orsino's page, disguised as a man) and the Malvolio subplot by Maria (Olivia's lady-in-waiting) (Figure 3.1). Viola's trajectory in the play is marked by rapid social advancement, culminating in her eventual marriage to Orsino. But that trajectory is directly tied to the work of domestic servitude. At the beginning of the play, she elects to enter service, first setting her sights upon Olivia, whom she has heard about from the sea captain ('O that I served that lady' [1.2.37]). The captain soon encourages her to shift her focus to Orsino, advising her to change her name to Cesario. As a page in Orsino's court, Viola/Cesario gains the privilege of access, intimacy, and mobility typical of only the best-positioned aristocratic servants, enabling her (for instance) to speak freely to both Olivia and Orsino. At times, Viola's role as a servant is so idealized, it becomes comic in its own right. At her first appearance at court, for example, Valentine tells her that '[i]f the Duke continue these favours towards you, Cesario, you are like to be much advanced. He hath known you but three days, and already you are no stranger' (1.4.1–4). Such a rapid rise in fortune contrasts sharply with the typical experience of young servants in Shakespeare's England, who often spent seven to ten years in service with little chance of mobility due to the prevalence of annual labour contracts.[20] Not only is Viola/Cesario's advantageous service position comically exaggerated, but she also explicitly rejects monetary payment in exchange for her service work. At the end of her first visit as a messenger to Olivia on behalf of Orsino, the countess offers her money, saying '[s]pend this for me' (1.5.273). But Viola responds by saying: 'I am no fee'd post, lady. Keep your purse. | My master, not myself, lacks recompense' (274–5). In this exchange, Viola shifts focus away from the economic context of the word 'recompense' in order to emphasize its emotional significance (i.e. that Olivia has refused to return Orsino's love for her). In doing

Figure 3.1 Olivia, Viola, and Maria from *Twelfth Night* (1.5). Painted by William Hamilton, R.A. and engraved by James Caldwall (1795). Courtesy of the Folger Shakespeare Library.

so, she also insists that her own work be located outside a money economy. Like her advantageous rise within the service hierarchy, Viola's pose of economic disinterestedness runs counter to the socio-economic realities of service for the majority of women in Shakespeare's England. Instead, the play encourages us to view Viola's service within a nostalgic, feudal model of allegiance, a framework that enables her to follow a path from service to marriage unencumbered by the messiness of contracts, wages, and other hallmarks of the capitalist service economy. In part, then, Shakespeare enables Viola to emerge as a romantic heroine by both alluding to and strategically erasing the economic realities of her service.

In *Twelfth Night*, the financial logic of service instead gets deflected onto other characters, notably Feste, who gets paid for his singing, and Olivia's lady-in-waiting, Maria. Like Viola, Maria is praised in the text for her wit, and she is often portrayed on stage as an authoritative, spunky woman with a mind of her own. Whereas Viola's service is divorced from crude financial motives or discussion of remuneration, however, Maria's actions are often described by others in explicitly economic language. Sir Toby, for instance, addresses Maria as his 'metal of India' (2.5.12–13), suggesting through a metaphor of global trade how valuable her crafty plotting is to him. Later in the same scene, he asserts that he is so enamoured with Maria's plot against Malvolio that he could marry her for it, asking 'no other dowry with her, but such another jest' (177–8). Of course, this is yet another romanticization, a fanciful version of the much more uncertain and difficult route from domestic service to marriage faced by the vast majority of early modern servants. But the emphasis on Maria's wit and skill as worthy of a dowry also recalls what we saw with Tranio in *The Taming of the Shrew*, namely, Shakespeare's depiction of the intelligent and crafty servant who acts independently and with a degree of improvisatory flair. As part of the plot that she concocts to make a fool of Malvolio, she drafts up some 'epistles of love' supposedly written to him by Olivia (2.3.149). She is able to pull this off because, as she tells Sir Toby and Sir Andrew: 'I can write very like my lady your [Sir Toby's] niece; on a forgotten matter we can hardly make distinction of our hands' (153–5). Although this deception is ultimately put to the side at the play's comic conclusion, it is a deception nonetheless, a subversion of the service hierarchy in which Maria skilfully performs the role of her mistress (much as Tranio did when wooing on behalf of Lucentio). In Maria's case, her witty and forthright actions temporarily confuse the status differential between mistress and servant, but they ultimately win her a marriage contract. As Fabian tells the court in the play's concluding scene, 'Maria writ | The letter, at Sir Toby's great importance [importunity], | In recompense whereof he hath married her' (5.1.359–61). Fabian's pronouncement reconnects the emotional and economic meanings of the word 'recompense' that Viola had earlier separated out from each other. For Maria, her wit does indeed become her dowry.[21]

In *Twelfth Night*, then, we can see Shakespeare creatively exploring different facets of women's service work in order to construct the characters of Viola and Maria and plot their comic trajectories. If Viola's romantic progression in the play relies upon an older model of service, Shakespeare shapes Maria's comic appeal—both to Sir Toby and to the audience—by instead building on a general understanding of women's (and women servants') skills and the economic value they bring with them to marriage. We see another indication of this in the figure of Olivia, whom Shakespeare presents throughout the play as a highly competent household manager. Olivia, Shakespeare suggests, is in part an attractive marital prospect not only because she is an heiress, but also because she is an able head of household. The wide-eyed Sebastian, who meets and is quickly wooed by Olivia late in the play, tells the audience that his strange experiences would lead him to believe that either he or Olivia had gone mad, except for the fact that:

> if 'twere so
> She could not sway her house, command her followers,
> Take and give back affairs and their dispatch
> With such a smooth, discreet, and stable bearing
> As I perceive she does. (4.3.16–20)

For Sebastian, Olivia's domestic competence and household leadership confirm the normality (rather than the madness) of the situation, and it is arguably these attributes that Sebastian finds erotically appealing. As is the case with Maria, Olivia's domestic skills help confirm her marriageability.[22] *Twelfth Night* thus offers a rich example of how Shakespeare could engage with women's domestic work as a fundamental component of his dramatic craft. In exploring both newer and older models of women's service, Shakespeare takes the traditional features of comic form and its push towards heterosexual marriage and reframes them through the lens of women's work.

Service, Race, and Slavery

By the turn of the seventeenth century, Shakespeare would certainly have been aware not only of the broader changes to the service economy that we've discussed so far, but also of the more specific category of slavery, particularly racialized slavery. Although the myth that slavery did not exist in England (including England in the early modern period) remained critical orthodoxy for many years, recent research has demonstrated that the enslavement of people of African descent did indeed occur in early modern England. Furthermore, ideas about slavery and bondage as they related to more generalized practices of service were very much central to the language, literatures, and general conduct of everyday English people, as Urvashi Chakravarty has shown.[23] In the 1550s, the first English ships brought enslaved black people directly from Africa, with many more arriving by the end of the century as England's participation in the international slave trade increased dramatically. And while 'Africans did not appear in English America until the second decade of the seventeenth century, slavery's widespread practice in Europe and Iberian America was by then common knowledge'.[24] As the pioneering research of Imtiaz Habib has demonstrated, England's participation in the slave trade has a much longer history than is often acknowledged, as it was often the case that 'black people in England endured a *de facto* slavery under the name of service' beginning in the sixteenth century.[25]

By the time that Shakespeare wrote *The Tempest* in 1610–11, he was unquestionably familiar with 'the categories and conditions of servitude and slavery practised daily in London and elsewhere in the British Isles'.[26] But even much earlier in his dramatic career, we can see Shakespeare exploring representations of slavery and the physicality of subservience. If we return for a moment, for instance, to *The Taming of the Shrew*, we can see an early example of the connection between servants and violence as a method of control. When we first meet Grumio, Petruchio's servant, he is engaged with his master in a playful series of verbal misunderstandings about the term 'knock' (Petruchio is asking Grumio to knock on the gate, but Grumio interprets Petruchio as asking him to hit ('knock') his master). When Grumio refuses, Petruchio '*wrings him by the ears*' (1.2.18). In a later scene, Grumio complains to Curtis of Petruchio's violent treatment, lamenting: 'Was ever man so beaten'? (4.1.2). As a character type, Grumio is modelled after enslaved figures from classical drama, who were often much abused (abuse that was played for comedic effect, as it is in *Shrew* as well). But as Patricia Akhimie has argued, the Shakespearian servant who suffers physical abuse—although not a direct marker of racial difference—was nevertheless evidence of 'pain or oppression that is justified in the eyes of a society by the presence of a stigmatized mark, located on the body'.[27] Akhimie discusses this process in *The Comedy of Errors*, another early comedy that features the identical twins Dromio of Antipholus and Dromio of Ephesus, enslaved brothers who are each physically abused by their masters. Dromio of Ephesus, for instance, complains that he has served his master 'from the hour of my nativity to this instant, and have nothing at his hands for my service but blows' (4.4.31–3). As Akhimie makes clear, the violence that continually marks the bodies of the two Dromios is a key part of how their subservience is made physically visible in the play. As she notes:

> The continual availability and vulnerability of servants' bodies to physical demands, including manual labor, and beatings, enabled both the household's economy and its hierarchy. The vulnerability and liminal position of servants, who bear the bruise and the abject status it represents, define the border of the English family and nation, both of which, as scholars have long argued, are central to the early modern understanding of race.[28]

Physical punishment may be aimed at correcting a servant's behaviour, but it also helps demarcate the 'relative worth of servants as human beings'.[29]

It is in *The Tempest*, however, where we see Shakespeare's most extensive engagement with service work in the form of racialized slavery. England's increased participation in global commerce in the early seventeenth century and the resulting development of global labour markets and, eventually, colonies led to its greater reliance on the Atlantic slave trade. *The Tempest* reflects this reality, even though its precise geographical setting is somewhat ambiguous: it is set on an island that seems to be located between Italy and North Africa, although many of the specific details of the play's setting (including the storm and shipwreck in the opening scene) are more suggestive of the new world (i.e. North America) rather than the old. As we learn in the play's opening act, Prospero and his daughter have been left marooned on this island twelve years prior, and they encountered there two specific inhabitants: Ariel, a 'spirit' who has some human attributes, and Caliban, the human son of the African woman Sycorax, who came to the island shortly before he was born. Even though Prospero does not arrive on the island as a colonizer per se, his actions 'fit the colonial paradigm: he appropriates the island's natural resources and makes Ariel his servant, Caliban his slave'.[30]

The contrasts Shakespeare draws between Ariel and Caliban in the text help distinguish the work of service from slavery, with the latter defined in explicitly racialized terms. Ariel, we learn, had been freed by Prospero from captivity in a 'cloven pine', a punishment given to him by Sycorax (whom Prospero calls a 'foul witch') (1.2.259, 278). When Prospero asks Ariel to perform 'more toil' for him at the beginning of the play, Ariel initially protests, reminding his master that he has done him 'worthy service' and has performed his duties '[w]ithout or grudge or grumblings'. As a result, Prospero had previously promised to release him from his labour contract a 'full year' early (1.2.243, 248–51). At least in theory, then, Ariel serves Prospero on a temporary basis, with the promise of eventual freedom. At the same time, Prospero threatens to renege on his promise if Ariel does not do the work requested of him, even suggesting he will reinstate the violent punishment originally put in place by Sycorax: 'If thou more murmur'st, I will rend an oak, | And peg thee in his knotty entrails till | Thou hast howled away twelve winters' (1.2.295–7). Prospero thus uses the threat of indefinite servitude to maintain control over Ariel until his own agendas (seeking revenge on his enemies, uniting his daughter Miranda and Ferdinand in marriage, and re-securing his political reputation) are met.[31]

By contrast, Caliban's service to Prospero is not depicted as contractual, but as enforced. Prospero introduces Caliban to the audience as 'my slave' and refers to him as such repeatedly throughout the play (1.2.310). Because he attempted sexual assault on Miranda, Caliban has been confined within a 'hard rock' (1.2.345) and denied liberty to move about the island (a stark contrast to Ariel's freedom of movement). Furthermore, Caliban is described in terms that mark him as racially distinct from the play's white Europeans. In the First Folio, the cast list identifies Caliban as a 'savage and deformed slave', and he is frequently called out by characters in the play for his physical difference: he is called a 'monster' around forty times, and Alonso exclaims that he is 'a strange thing as e'er I looked on' (5.1.292–3).[32] In addition, as many scholars have noted, Caliban's name is a near anagram of 'cannibal', which may have suggested his African origins, given that many Europeans were appalled by rumours of supposed cannibalism by African peoples. The implication of cannibalism may likewise have signalled Caliban's links to native American peoples, who were also accused in European treatises and illustrations of eating human flesh.[33] As Virginia Mason Vaughan and Alden T. Vaughan summarize: 'If English readers and viewers saw Caliban as an American Indian, an African, or a fusion of the two ancestries, he reflected the widely held conviction on both sides of the Atlantic that those people were inherently dark, savage, and eminently suitable for slavery.'[34] We see these connections to racialized slavery born out in the text, as Caliban is (for instance) 'pinched' and made to suffer 'cramps' and 'side-stitches' by Prospero when he shows signs of insubordination (1.2.330, 326–7). Similar to the bruises endured by the enslaved Dromios in *The Comedy of Errors*, these bodily marks, as Akhimie has demonstrated, reinforce his unfree status and confirm his fundamentally 'base' nature.[35]

At the same time, Shakespeare provides ample evidence in the play of the value of Caliban's labour to Prospero, which includes many of the domestic duties necessary to maintain a household. As Prospero reminds Miranda: 'We cannot miss him. He does make our fire, | Fetch in our wood, and serves in offices | That profit us' (1.2.313–15). Caliban's enforced service is essential to Prospero's and Miranda's survival on the island, but the labour that he performs is as degrading as it is indispensable. In contrast to Ferdinand who, as we discussed in the Introduction, also performs the labour of carrying logs onstage, Caliban's labour is enforced and ongoing, and it does not hold out to him the promise of transformation or reward, as it does for Ferdinand.[36] Instead, it marks him as a base labourer who is incapable of the kinds of social mobility and ingenuity we see in servants such as Tranio in *The Taming of the Shrew* or Maria in *Twelfth Night*. To be sure, Shakespeare provides a kind of critique of enforced labour through Caliban himself, who often speaks with eloquence and beauty throughout the play and who asserts his own claim to the island while demonstrating his mastery of 'subsistence survival skills'.[37] Indeed, it is in part through the tension between Caliban's autonomy and his enforced subservience that *The Tempest* displays its profound, if uneasy engagement with emerging understandings of race and enslavement. In doing so, the play provides a vivid example of how Shakespeare's staging of service was deeply informed by emerging practices of racialized slavery in a global context. Like the depictions of service we have examined throughout this chapter, Shakespeare's dramatization of Ariel and Caliban in *The Tempest* demonstrates how he transformed the historical conditions of the early modern service economy into the materials of dramatic action, characterization, and thematic exploration. The result is a deft exploration across a range of genres of the nature of power, social order, and even the very definition of what it means to be human.

Shakespeare and Work. Michelle M. Dowd, Oxford University Press. © Michelle M. Dowd 2026.
DOI: 10.1093/9780191998096.003.0004

4

Artisans and Apprentices

Artisans and apprentices are not quite as ubiquitous on Shakespeare's stage as are the servants discussed in Chapter 3. However, these workers do play key roles in several major plays and references to their work permeate Shakespeare's language throughout his canon. Examining the varied roles of apprentices and artisans, this chapter argues that Shakespeare—an artisan in his own right, as we saw in Chapter 2—draws deeply on the social and economic circumstances of early modern craftspeople to construct not only memorable characters, but also highly resonant dramatic imagery. Beginning with a section that provides some background about the work of early modern apprentices and artisans, the chapter then examines how Shakespeare represents these figures in a range of dramatic genres. We will consider plays such as *Julius Caesar*, *Coriolanus*, *A Midsummer Night's Dream*, and *2 Henry VI*, to trace how artisans and their labour help shape Shakespeare's theatrical storytelling. In the final section of the chapter, we will focus attention more specifically on the language of apprentices and other manual labourers in plays such as *Titus Andronicus* where these workers are otherwise absent from the stage. By considering not only staged representations, but also theatrical imagery, we will see how Shakespeare deployed certain kinds of 'working words' to explore such important topics as social unrest and violence.

Apprentices, Artisans, and Craft Work in Shakespeare's England

What did it mean to be an apprentice or an artisan worker in late sixteenth- and early seventeenth-century England? In broad terms, these workers were engaged in some type of manual labour that took the form of a distinct craft or trade. Their numbers were highest in urban settings (London in particular), where they represented a wide range of small trades and crafts that suited the diversified economies of early modern English towns. Crafts with which Shakespeare would have been familiar included feltmakers, weavers, shoemakers, carpenters, smiths, and pinmakers, as well as more lucrative trades such as goldsmithing and shipbuilding.[1] In the Induction to *The Taming of the Shrew*, as we saw in Chapter 1, Christopher Sly gives us a quick overview of his varied occupational history, which includes several of these small trades. He tells the Lord who questions him that he is 'by birth a pedlar, by education a cardmaker, by transmutation a bearherd, and now by present profession a tinker?' (Induction 2.12, 13, 16–20). In this case, Sly's working life has been an itinerant and unstable one, defined not in terms of a stable 'career', but according to a series of crafts taken up in succession.

Sly's experiences mirrored the reality for many in Shakespeare's England. But in its ideal form, those working in crafts would follow a clear trajectory that led them from apprenticeship to independent artisanal work. Like the domestic servants discussed in Chapter 3, most apprentices in the period were in their late teens or early twenties when they began their terms. Unlike servants, apprentices were not paid wages, but were instead entered into a contract to train with and work for an individual master for a set term, usually seven years. Indeed, families often had to pay premiums to a master in order to enter their children into apprenticeships. In exchange, apprentices would typically live in their master's house and learn a craft or trade, with the goal of eventually becoming economically independent. During their indenture, apprentices would learn a range of skills appropriate to their specific trade, including the proper handling of tools and a thorough understanding of raw materials.[2] Both women and men became apprentices, but during Shakespeare's lifetime the opportunities for women were quite limited (this would change in the second half of the seventeenth century).[3] As a result, most apprentices were young men, a reality reflected in Shakespeare's plays, as we'll see. Even so, apprentices represented a very large part of the population in early modern England. As Ilana Krausman Ben-Amos notes:

> About 1,400 youths began apprenticeship terms every year in mid-sixteenth century London, comprising, together with those already apprenticed in the

> town, about one-tenth of the capital's population within the walls at this time. By the early years of the seventeenth century their numbers had more than doubled.[4]

Another historian has estimated that 'two thirds of *all* men in sixteenth-century London served apprenticeships' at some point in their lives—an extraordinary number that gives a sense of just how widespread the apprenticeship system was.[5]

When an apprentice's term was up, they would usually enter the workforce proper, either as a journeyman who worked for wages (sometimes remaining in the same shop and household with the same master) or as a craftsperson or retailer who ran their own shop. Journeymen had a higher social standing than apprentices, and the fact that they earned wages meant that they had greater economic independence too, even if they still often depended on their master for room and board. The end of apprenticeship also brought about another major milestone for these workers: admission as a member of the company to which they had been apprenticed. Once an apprentice had completed their indenture period in full, they could be sworn in at the Guildhall as a citizen or 'freeman' of London. Although there were a few other routes to citizenship (such as making a claim to citizen status by patrimony or receiving it as a gift from the crown), the vast majority—nine out of every ten men in sixteenth-century London—became citizens through apprenticeship. What was so significant about being a citizen? As historian Steve Rappaport explains, citizenship was a prerequisite for full participation in early modern economic life. Being a citizen (or possessing the 'freedom' as it was also known) was not just an honorific. Instead, citizenship usually entailed membership in a livery company (a type of guild that dated back to the medieval period) and it granted individuals the right to engage independently in economic activity, including any form of trade. The livery companies played a central role in organizing early modern urban life and regulating its labour practices. Some of the most notable companies in Shakespeare's day were the Clothworkers, the Drapers, the Grocers, the Merchant Taylors, the Brewers, and the Carpenters, to name just a few. The company system provided a process by which a worker could move from apprenticeship to journeyman (or independent wage labourer) and then potentially on to a position as a master of a given craft or trade. Of course, many apprentices did not complete their terms, and others ended up finding employment in trades that were different from those for which they apprenticed. Nevertheless, the livery company system offered a clear structure and well-defined pathway for training workers to become skilled artisans in a specific craft or trade.[6]

As we saw in Chapter 1, the theatre was connected to the livery company system and artisanal work in important ways. Many of the professional players in London's theatres were members of livery companies and would have brought their personal experiences and direct knowledge of apprenticeship and artisanal labour with them to the commercial theatres. In addition, the professional theatres themselves were based on a guild model of labour. Adult actors and sharers in a playing company would often take on boys as apprentices to play women's roles and other parts in order to hone their theatrical craft.[7] Playwrights too, and Shakespeare in particular, were directly connected to artisanal labour. As we saw in Chapter 2, Shakespeare was raised in an artisanal household, and he would have been familiar with the daily work of craftspeople from his experiences growing up as the son of a glover. Furthermore, writing plays, as Chapter 2 discusses, was understood as a craft in the period. As an 'artisan-playwright', Shakespeare would have been well aware of the work of apprentices and artisans both in and beyond the professional theatre.[8]

Apprentices and artisans were connected to the theatre in another important way as well: as audience members. The evidence we have suggests that these workers attended plays regularly in the period, especially plays staged at the larger public amphitheatres, at times comprising a significant segment of the audience. The presence of these workers in theatrical audiences contributed to the 'dynamics of the amphitheatre as a relatively pluralistic public space' that fostered a variety of perspectives and personal responses.[9] But their presence also raised concerns about violence and social unrest. Antitheatricalist writers, such as Stephen Gosson and others, expressed concerns about 'idle' artisans who might skip work to attend a play, and they warned about the disruptions that could be caused by large groups of artisans or apprentices who came to the theatre as playgoers. Indeed, there were several historical incidents in which young apprentices as well as craftsmen acted collectively and violently against the theatres themselves, most notably during the Shrovetide holiday period preceding Lent.[10] We will explore this intersection of craft work, the early modern theatre, and violence in more detail later in this chapter. But for now, it's worth noting two things that will be important in our analysis of Shakespeare's engagement with craft work in his plays: (1) the association of apprentices and artisans with violence (real or imagined) was a common one; and (2) that association did not necessarily imply a uniformly negative judgment of these workers on the part of playwrights or players.[11] Instead, as we will see, Shakespeare's representation of apprentices and craft workers was complex and multifaceted, and it shaped the dramatic texture of his plays in significant ways.

Artisanal Labour on Shakespeare's Stage

Shakespeare's plays may not initially seem like the most obvious places to look for artisanal characters or scenes of apprentice labour, in part because he did not set his plays in contemporary London, as many of his fellow playwrights did. Dramatists such as Thomas Heywood, Thomas Middleton, and Thomas Dekker, for instance, often staged craftspeople and apprentices at work, usually in comedic plots. In his popular *The Shoemaker's Holiday*, for instance, Dekker depicts several scenes featuring apprentice and journeymen shoemakers, in addition to scenes that highlight women's retail work in a sempster's (or tailoring) shop. Shakespeare's plays do not set their sights so directly on the immediate economic milieu of London. However, Shakespeare nevertheless populates his plays with highly memorable artisanal characters. And he also drew inspiration from craft workers throughout his oeuvre, often not by staging these figures directly, but by bringing the world and context they inhabited vividly to life through his dramatic language.

An early scene in *1 Henry IV* provides a good example of Shakespeare's incorporation of artisans and apprentices into the dramatic fabric of his plays. Speaking with Ned Poins at an inn in Eastcheap, Prince Hal boasts that he spent some time with several tapsters (or 'drawers') and got to know them so well that he can 'call them all by their christen names' (2.5.7–8). In addition, Hal has learned their distinct figures of speech, leading him to conclude triumphantly: 'I am so good a proficient in one quarter of an hour that I can drink with any tinker in his own language during my life' (17–19). Hal characterizes his offstage interactions with these workers in terms of linguistic ability; by associating with lower-status workers like tapsters (something his father, King Henry, would never do), Hal seeks to develop a better understanding of his future subjects. For Hal, that understanding (as flawed as it may be) derives not from shared work or class status, but from his own agile appropriation of the distinctive *language* of craft workers. Immediately following his speech to Poins, Hal calls for the apprentice tapster Francis and torments him with questions in order 'to drive away the time' until Falstaff returns (2.5.27). During this exchange, Hal sends Poins offstage and asks him to call repeatedly for Francis so that the apprentice is pulled verbally in two directions at the same time, to comic effect. The (frequently interrupted) onstage exchange hinges on the terms of Francis's apprenticeship as a drawer:

> PRINCE HARRY Come hither, Francis.
> FRANCIS My Lord.
> PRINCE HARRY How long hast thou to serve, Francis?
> FRANCIS Forsooth, five years, and as much as to—
> POINS (*within*) Francis!
> FRANCIS Anon, anon, sir!
> PRINCE HARRY Five year! By'r Lady, a long lease for
> the clinking of pewter. But Francis, darest thou be so
> valiant as to play the coward with thy indenture, and
> show it a fair pair of heels, and run from it? (2.5.38–47)

Francis appears to be five years into what would typically have been a seven-year indenture period for apprentices. But Hal is less interested in the details of Francis's work than he is in goading him about the terms of his apprenticeship and whether he might 'be so valiant' as to break his indenture and leave his master. Keeping Francis awkwardly balanced between going and coming, Hal mimics the temporary, yet prolonged, structures of economic dependence that marked the apprenticeship system. And while he also seems to encourage Francis to reject his own master, Hal himself retains full mastery over the scene, where he holds an unquestioned position of authority as both a prince and a customer in the inn. Hal's playful, if cruel, manipulation of Francis in this episode is thus deeply indebted to his awareness of apprenticeship as a distinctive form of labour. In the process, the scene helps provide the audience with a greater understanding of the prince's character, including both his populist impulses and his less appealing tendencies towards condescension.

However, it is in a play written just a year or two earlier than *1 Henry IV* that Shakespeare presents us with some of his most memorable artisan characters. In *A Midsummer Night's Dream*, as we saw briefly in the Introduction, Shakespeare introduces us to a lively group of so-called 'mechanicals' who are rehearsing a play to perform at Duke Theseus' upcoming wedding. The term 'mechanical' explicitly meant an artisan, a worker who performed manual labour.[12] The stage direction at the beginning of Act 1, scene 2 clearly identifies each of these characters according to their occupations: '*Enter Quince the carpenter, and Snug the joiner, and Bottom the weaver, and Flute the bellows-mender, and Snout the tinker, and Starveling the tailor.*' Certainly, this group of amateur thespians functions as 'low' comic relief with the play's larger romantic-comedic arc, providing a delightful contrast to the more elite world of the human lovers from Athens and the magical world of the fairies. But while both their scenes of rehearsal and their closing performance of *Pyramus and Thisbe* invite laughter and even a degree of derision, their creative energy is nevertheless central to the play and its comic resolution. And that energy is directly connected to their status as artisans.

Bottom and his fellow craftsmen have long been understood by critics of the play as central rather than subordinate to its major themes. But the presence of these 'mechanicals' onstage in the 1590s would have also invoked some specific, real-world concerns about artisans and social unrest. Bottom's occupation as a weaver, for instance, would have had particular social significance at the time *A Midsummer Night's Dream* was written and first performed. This period in England was one of notable economic hardships, marked by bad harvests as well as frequent riots on the part of apprentices and artisans, especially clothmakers. Many of these riots were directed against 'strangers', or foreign workers in England who were accused of 'causing unemployment, a decline in trade, and a rise in prices'.[13] A large number of these riots, led mostly by workers in the cloth trade, occurred between 1590 and 1596, and so would have been very current to playgoers first attending a performance of *A Midsummer Night's Dream*.[14] The presence of artisan characters such as Bottom in the play thus highlights broader class tensions and concerns about the potential disorderliness of lowborn workers in sixteenth-century England.

However, the violence that the mechanicals' occupations might have suggested to Shakespeare's audiences never materializes in the play, at least not directly. In fact, while rehearsing their play, these artisans go comically out of their way to avoid even the hint of violence in their performance. Bottom first raises a concern about the violence of *Pyramus and Thisbe* to his fellow artisan-actors in Act 3:

> BOTTOM There are things in this comedy of Pyramus and Thisbe that will never please. First, Pyramus must draw a sword to kill himself, which the ladies cannot abide. How answer you that?
> SNOUT By'r la'kin, a parlous fear.
> STARVELING I believe we must leave the killing out, when all is done.
> BOTTOM Not a whit. I have a device to make all well. Write me a prologue, and let the prologue seem to say we will do no harm with our swords, and that Pyramus is not killed indeed; and for the more better assurance, tell them that I, Pyramus, am not Pyramus, but Bottom the weaver. This will put them out of fear. (3.1.8–20)

The threat of deadly violence is raised only to be softened and deflected. Bottom suggests the paratextual device of the prologue, a strategy that is eventually adopted by the troupe, to mitigate the perceived danger of their story. But he also singles out his own occupation as a weaver as further grounds for reassurance. Though this exchange and its eventual performance is ludicrous in theatrical terms, it cleverly manages to redefine the figure of the artisan-weaver not as a potential source of riot or violence, but as a comforting figure that promises familiarity and even safety. Rather than representing the artisans as potentially violent, in *A Midsummer Night's Dream*

Shakespeare, as Theodore Leinwand has argued, displaces that lawlessness onto the 'disobedient and violent lovers' of the main plot.[15]

Instead, Shakespeare presents the mechanicals to us in largely positive, if often laughable, terms. Rather than signalling violence, these artisans display passion, dedication, and good-natured commitment to their (albeit highly amateur) theatrical craft. Despite their clear identification in the text according to their occupations, the only labour we actually see Bottom and his companions perform onstage is the work of rehearsing and performing *Pyramus and Thisbe* for Theseus and Hippolyta's nuptials. The play thus directly invokes their labour as artisans while also transforming it into the work of theatre-making. To be sure, Shakespeare consistently draws attention to the mechanicals' lack of refinement and their naivety about theatrical practice. For instance, Quince chastises Flute during rehearsal by noting his inability to follow the cue script properly: 'You speak all your part at once, cues and all' (3.1.93–4). But at the same time, Shakespeare emphasizes the energy and passion these 'hempen homespuns' (a phrase that Robin uses to describe them) (3.1.71) bring to their theatrical pursuits. Bottom in particular is, from his very first appearance in the play, notable for his energy, action, and passion, even to the point of excess. As Peter Quince provides the details of plot and character that constitute *Pyramus and Thisbe*, Bottom eagerly asserts his willingness to play all of the necessary roles in the tragedy. In his assertion that he will call up tears 'in the true performing' of his roles, he likewise promises to move the audience to passion: 'I will move stones' (1.2.22–3). Bottom's enthusiasm may be infectious, but it also marks him as potentially unrefined and lacking in self-control, qualities that were often associated with non-elite working men. But if Bottom's excessive vigour in rehearsal indicates his low status, it also underscores the potential appeal and creativity made possible through the body of the artisan labourer—a man who might literally 'move stones' through industrious labour as well as touch the hearts of an audience.

Bottom's fellow artisans, certainly, have nothing but praise for him. Quince assures Bottom that he is the best choice to play Pyramus, because he is a 'sweet-faced man; a proper man as one shall see in a summer's day; a most lovely, gentlemanlike man'. Therefore, he concludes, Bottom 'must needs play Pyramus' (1.2.80–2). Later, the men fear that their theatrical labour will be lost entirely if Bottom cannot be found. Quince insists that it will not be possible to put on the play without him because there is 'not a man in all Athens able to discharge Pyramus but he' (4.2.7–8). Flute agrees, adding that 'sweet bully Bottom' 'hath simply the best wit of any handicraft-man in Athens' (4.2.18, 9–10). If we take the words of Bottom's companions at face value, rather than relying exclusively on the judgements of the play's Athenian aristocrats, a picture emerges of a capable, even handsome artisan who is a hard-working (if not necessarily highly talented) actor as well.[16] The play's rehearsal scenes, as Tom Rutter has argued, are more than just low-comic interludes. For all of their light-heartedness, they also 'emphasize to the audience the labour that has gone into the performance they are watching'.[17] Bottom's effervescence in the rehearsal sequences thus suggests the creative force of artisan labour vis-à-vis the early modern theatre. Shakespeare brings together labour and inspiration by capitalizing on the productive capacity of artisanal work.

Of course, when we get to Act 5 and the outlandish performance of *Pyramus and Thisbe* that is so soundly ridiculed by Duke Theseus and the other aristocrats, it may seem easy to dismiss the mechanicals and separate out the 'true' work of theatrical performance from their amateurish efforts. However, such an approach underestimates the significance of Bottom and his fellow artisans to the creative, theatrical world of this comedy. When Theseus asks about the identity of the actors who have come to perform *Pyramus and Thisbe*, Egeus tells him that they are:

> Hard-handed men that work in Athens here,
> Which never laboured in their minds till now,
> And now have toiled their unbreathed memories
> With this same play against your nuptial. (5.1.72–5)

Egeus' speech is certainly meant to be dismissive, emphasizing as it does the contrast between manual labour and the labour of the mind required for theatrical performance. But at the same time, even Egeus' derogatory speech highlights the continuity between the mechanicals' unskilled labour and what he imagines to be the more refined labour of acting. Egeus repeatedly invokes the category of 'work' to describe not only the mechanicals' menial occupations, but also their performance of the play at hand. And though the verb 'toiled' is meant to ridicule the forced nature of the mechanicals' performance, it also suggests that performing *Pyramus and Thisbe* is difficult work. As Rutter notes, Egeus here (perhaps inadvertently) makes clear the 'mental labour—memorizing lines and rehearsing their delivery—that goes into even the worst of plays'.[18] Despite Egeus' intentions, then, the passage makes explicit the connection between artisanal labour and the labour of theatre.

And what is more, neither Egeus' disparaging comments nor the critiques levied against the performers by their onstage aristocratic audience can erase the fact that for the broader audience sitting in the playhouse watching *A Midsummer Night's Dream*, the mechanicals' performance of *Pyramus and Thisbe*, a performance solidly dependent on artisan labour, dominates the action of Act 5 and provides what are arguably its most delightful and indelible moments. In his depiction of the mechanicals' trajectory from artisan workers to rehearsing artists to performing actors, Shakespeare suggests that theatrical enterprise depends upon craft work for its creative spark. The theatre, that is, offers a continuum between work and play, between labour and creativity. Through the figures of Bottom and his fellow artisans, Shakespeare highlights the latent creative potential of the early modern artisan and implicitly redefines the theatre not as an escape from work, as many of the antitheatricalists charged (as we saw in Chapter 1), but as an imaginative extension of it.

Staging Crowds, Labour, and Violence

In *A Midsummer Night's Dream*, violence is alluded to but ultimately dissociated from the actual artisans we see onstage, who are presented in largely positive and even upbeat terms linked with theatrical creativity. Elsewhere, however, we see Shakespeare engaged much more explicitly with issues of artisanal violence and with popular concerns about the dangerous unruliness of apprentices and craft workers. Often these moments involve crowds, with their focus on groups of labourers rather than on individuals. There is a legal basis for this connection between crowds and violence in early modern England: in addition to the seriousness of the threat posed, the size of the group was a key component in determining whether or not an expression of collective violence was defined as a 'riot' and, if it was, how harshly those involved were punished.[19] Legally then, as well as in the public imagination more broadly, collective groups of workers were much more threatening than individuals acting alone. And the theatre was a particularly rich and potentially explosive place to consider these threats, given that most audience members would have come from what we might now think of as the 'working classes' and because the act of playgoing itself 'turns individuals into collectives'.[20] Going to the theatre means becoming part of a crowd, after all. As we'll see, apprentices and artisans often enter the world of Shakespeare's plays as either explicitly or obliquely threatening collectives, and they infuse these texts and performances with an energy that is directly tied to historical concerns about the relationship between craft labourers and violence, whether real or imagined.

Julius Caesar provides one good example of Shakespeare depicting artisans *en masse* and highlighting their unruliness. Although this play is set in ancient Rome, the commoners depicted in its opening scene, a group that includes a carpenter and a cobbler, among others, bear a strong resemblance to English artisans. Certainly, Flavius and Murellus, the two tribunes of the people, admonish the commoners in terms that would have been well known to English audiences, invoking fears about idleness and a lack of productive work. In the lines that open the play, Flavius speaks to the crowd:

> Hence, home, you idle creatures, get you home!
> Is this a holiday? What, know you not,
> Being mechanical, you ought not walk
> Upon a labouring day without the sign
> Of your profession?—Speak, what trade art thou? (1.1.1–5)

The word 'mechanical' reminds us of Bottom and his fellow artisans in *A Midsummer Night's Dream*, indicating that the group consists of handicraftsmen. Flavius' primary concern, however, is the *lack* of work these men are doing: they are walking about the streets 'idle' on a working day. Time, in other words, is marked by labour (or the lack thereof), and these men are violating accepted rules that govern the temporality of work.[21] For the tribunes, the idleness of this carpenter, cobbler, and their fellow artisans is directly linked to a concern about their mobility and their presence as a restless crowd out on the public streets. As Flavius asks the Cobbler: 'But wherefore art not in thy shop today? |

Why dost thou lead these men about the streets'? (27–8). Although violence is not invoked directly here, the scene clearly establishes a connection between 'idle' artisans, public crowds, and the potential for unease and social unrest. The scene also invites Shakespeare's audience members to draw comparisons between these ostensibly Roman workers and unruly crowds much closer to home. When Murellus chastises the gathered workers, calling them 'blocks' and 'stones' and 'worse than senseless things' (1.1.35), he describes them as a mass of people gathering in the streets, an image that brings to mind, as John Archer has argued, 'other descriptions of teeming streets and crowded windows in Shakespeare, like Bolingbroke's entry into London in *Richard II*'.[22] It also may bring to mind the crowds of audience members at theatres such as the Globe, just as the tribune's concern about these 'mechanicals' leaving work to roam the streets mirrors the Elizabethan fear about artisans skipping work to attend the theatre.

In other plays, as we saw in *A Midsummer Night's Dream*, Shakespeare alludes to real, historical artisanal rebellions that would have been prominent in the cultural consciousness of the day. In *All is True* (*Henry VIII*), the Duke of Norfolk responds to Queen Katherine's concerns about 'loud rebellion' by describing an uprising of craftspeople who are protesting against taxation and hunger:

> for upon these taxations
> The clothiers all, not able to maintain
> The many to them 'longing, have put off
> The spinsters, carders, fullers, weavers, who,
> Unfit for other life, compelled by hunger
> And lack of other means, in desperate manner
> Daring th'event to th' teeth, are all in uproar,
> And danger serves among them. (1.2.31–8)

In Norfolk's speech, Shakespeare draws on a description of a local rebellion taken from Holinshed's *Chronicles* (1587), in which wealthy clothiers assent to taxes, but are forced to lay off other workers. Shakespeare here exaggerates the violence of the rebellion for dramatic effect (to potentially demonstrate, among other things, King Henry's political impotence in this scene). More prominently, in *Coriolanus*, Shakespeare opens the play with a vivid invocation of recent Elizabethan hunger riots, again (as in *Julius Caesar*) despite the

Roman setting.[23] The play begins with the entrance of a '*company of mutinous Citizens*' (1.1.1 s.d.). When Menenius enters and asks the citizens what they are doing, they assert that they plan to take their 'strong arms' and wield them against the patricians, who they angrily claim: 'suffer us to famish, and their storehouses crammed with grain' (1.1.58, 78–9). As scholars have argued, Shakespeare here alludes to the recent Midlands Rising of 1607, which occurred just two years before he likely started writing *Coriolanus*. The revolt was primarily instigated by workers angry about the enclosure of common land (a topic we will return to in Chapter 5), but it is clear from historical documents that food shortages were also a significant issue for the protesters.[24] Coriolanus is notoriously dismissive of the play's citizens, whom he identifies specifically as craftsmen by referring to them as 'Rome's mechanics' (5.3.84). Similar to the St Crispian's Day speech delivered by King Henry in *Henry V* discussed in the Introduction, Coriolanus in this exchange gives precedence to the work of warfare rather than the work of artisans.[25] Shakespeare thus draws upon recent incidents of collective violence on the part of craft workers to set the stage for Coriolanus' contemptuous treatment of the plebians, a key factor in his self-identification as a military leader and, ultimately, a cause of his downfall.

Shakespeare treats artisan rebels more extensively and with more nuance in *2 Henry VI* (likely written around 1591), another play that draws on real-life popular protests for inspiration. Although the historical rebellion that the play takes as its most obvious source is Jack Cade's rebellion of 1450, a popular anti-government revolt, it is clear that Shakespeare freely blended several different historical events together when creating his fictional Cade and his fellow rebels. Shakespeare linked together the Peasant's Revolt of 1381, Cade's rebellion, and more recent uprisings such as the so-called Evil May Day revolt in 1517 (when apprentices attacked foreign workers in London) and the protests led by clothworkers in the 1590s discussed previously.[26] In its focus on the domestic political disputes that led up to the Wars of the Roses, *2 Henry VI*, not surprisingly, makes civil unrest its central theme. However, the attention given to the rebels throughout the play creates a backdrop of civil unrest that is grounded not only in aristocratic disputes, but also in the popular protests of artisan workers.

Before we are even introduced to Cade, we are provided with another scene of apprentice protest and violence that is focused on an individual rather than a collective. In the play's opening act, we are introduced to Peter Thump, an armorer's apprentice, who has accused his master, Horner, of treasonously proclaiming the Duke of York (rather than Henry) as the 'rightful heir to the crown' (1.3.28–9). In the following act, Peter and Horner fight in single combat to resolve the dispute, as ordered by Gloucester. The scene is a parody of the traditional chivalric trial by combat, with Horner, for instance, arriving drunk. But it ends with Horner's death at the hands of Peter, a violent incident of petty treason that is left unresolved in the play. And although Peter fights alone, he is cheered on by several apprentices, one of whom encourages him to 'be merry, Peter, and fear not thy master. Fight for credit of the prentices!' (2.3.74–5). The scene thus conjures up images of popular riots and apprentices banding together as a group, the kind of communal identity that could lead to violence in the popular imagination. But while the exchange takes the audience to the verge of working-class violence *en masse*, it stops short of the full realization of that violence by narrowing its scope. Rather than invoking images of violent crowds, the scene keeps its focus on one—highly reluctant and frightened—individual apprentice who fights his master under duress as a direct response to treason. Furthermore, Peter's violence, though potentially quite disruptive of social order, is ultimately sanctioned in the play, both by the legitimacy of his accusations (Horner cries out as he dies: 'I confess, I confess treason' [2.3.98]) and by direct royal approval (King Henry says that the duel has revealed Peter's 'truth and innocence' [2.3.107]).[27]

Peter's mock-epic violence against his master sets the stage for the insurrection led by Jack Cade later in the play, a much more dangerous challenge to the social order than the comedic exchanges between Peter and Horner, despite the fatal results of their duel. Like Bottom in *A Midsummer Night's Dream*, Cade's character is an artisan 'during a time of economic hardship that inspired frequent protests and riots'. And like Bottom, Cade is also a clothworker (a shearman) during a period in which clothmakers were often associated with popular protests.[28] But in other respects, Shakespeare's Cade couldn't be more different from the 'sweet bully Bottom' (*Midsummer* 4.2.18). Most significantly, Cade commands a powerful and threatening presence onstage. He and his fellow artisans take the violent potential that was merely hinted at by the mechanicals in *A Midsummer Night's Dream* and make it a reality: Cade kills Sir Humphrey Stafford and his brother William as well as Lord Saye (among other victims), and he and his men march on London before eventually disbanding (Figure 4.1). Cade is associated with violence even before he appears onstage; in describing Cade in battle against the Irish, the Duke of York notes that he 'fought so long till that his thighs with darts | Were almost like a sharp-quilled porcupine' (3.1.362–3). And later in the play, Shakespeare explicitly connects the violence of the rebels with their artisanal trades. Take the following exchange when the rebels gather to plot their rebellion:

> SECOND REBEL There's Best's son, the tanner of Wingham—
> FIRST REBEL He shall have the skins of our enemies to make dog's leather of.
> SECOND REBEL And Dick the butcher—
> FIRST REBEL Then is sin struck down like an ox, and iniquity's throat cut like a calf.
> SECOND REBEL And Smith the weaver—
> FIRST REBEL Argo, their thread of life is spun. (4.2.23–31)

Not only do the men comprise a threatening collective force, but their specific occupational skills as artisans (in this case as tanners, butchers, and weavers) provide the imaginative grounds for the acts of violence they plan to commit. Indeed, in the following scene, following the death of the Staffords, Cade commends the butcher for his prowess, exclaiming: 'They fell before thee like sheep and oxen, and thou behaved'st thyself as if thou hadst been in thine own slaughterhouse' (4.3.3–5). As Ronda Arab notes of these lines, the 'connection between artisanal work and violent artisanal power could not be made clearer'.[29]

And yet, Shakespeare's representation of Cade is not entirely negative. Cade's brutality and anarchic energy certainly mark him as a villain in the play. He threatens political upheaval, while also himself being a political hypocrite: he tells his followers that 'all things will be in common', but he nevertheless seeks to rule over others and asserts that 'the proudest peer in the realm shall not wear a head on his

Figure 4.1 Jack Cade and Lord Say from *2 Henry VI* (4.7). Drawn by William Ralston and engraved by R. S. Marriott (1863–75). Courtesy of the Folger Shakespeare Library.

shoulders unless he pay me tribute' (4.7.17, 117–18). At the same time, his physical prowess is admired by many in the play, and his dynamic physicality would have no doubt appealed to many in the playhouse as well. Similarly, Cade's critique of social inequality would almost certainly have resonated with fellow artisans and lower-class members of Shakespeare's audiences. When Stafford questions Cade about his occupation in an attempt to belittle him, Cade's response seems designed to elicit cheers from both his followers and, likely, many playgoers:

> STAFFORD Villain, thy father was a plasterer
> And thou thyself a shearman, art thou not?
> CADE And Adam was a gardener. (4.2.131–3)

Cade's cheeky response to Stafford validates lower-order work and celebrates artisans as foundational to English social order. It also would have reminded audiences of John Ball's speech during the Peasant's Revolt of 1381 (retold in Holinshed's *Chronicles*), in which he famously asked: when Adam delve and Eve span, who was then a gentleman? It is not hard to imagine Elizabethan audiences agreeing, at least in part, with Cade's commentary on social order and inequality, despite his brutality elsewhere in the play. By drawing positively on the language of manual labour, Shakespeare adds depth to Cade's character and challenges the audience to think critically about the causes of social unrest.[30]

'Clubs, Clubs!': Artisanal Language and Violence

As we've seen, Shakespeare's complex, even ambivalent, portrayal of artisans in *2 Henry VI* draws not only on the onstage presence of Cade and his compatriots, but also on language that powerfully suggests a connection between specific occupations (such as butchers and weavers) and social violence. In the First Rebel's simile, for instance, that 'iniquity's throat' will be 'cut like a calf', he offers up a play on words that highlights the poetic utility of artisanal language for Shakespeare. When craft labour is embedded within his figurative language, Shakespeare can draw on its range of socio-economic associations to amplify or complicate his dramatic plots, even when he chooses not to stage such labour directly. In *2 Henry VI*, Shakespeare connects the rebels to violence by verbally emphasizing their positions as artisanal workers, even before they engage in onstage combat. In this final section, I want to explore Shakespeare's suggestive use of the language of artisanal and apprentice labour further, with a focus on one specific example: the word 'clubs'.

We can start tracing the significance of 'clubs' (as a word and an object) to Shakespeare's representation of artisans by returning to the opening scene of *Coriolanus*. The company of 'mutinous citizens' that enters, as we learn from the opening stage direction, comes onto the stage with '*staves, clubs, and other weapons*' (1.1.1 s.d.). A few lines into the scene, Menenius asks them, 'Where go you | With bats and clubs?' (53–4), adding verbal emphasis to the visible onstage objects. The text's identification of these particular props is hardly arbitrary: clubs and cudgels were weapons specifically associated with apprentice riots in the period. They were used, for instance, during many of the Shrovetide riots, in which many apprentices and craft workers participated.[31] This context is fitting for 'Rome's mechanics' (5.3.84) in *Coriolanus*, but a similar reference to clubs in *Romeo and Juliet* seems to invite a different set of associations. In the opening scene of the tragedy, after Benvolio and Tybalt begin fighting, the stage direction indicates: '*Enter three or four Citizens, with clubs or partisans*' (1.1.69 s.d.). Upon entering, these citizens shout out: 'Clubs, bills and partisans! Strike! Beat them down! | Down with the Capulets. Down with the Montagues' (1.1.70–1). The citizens in this instance are most likely civic guards or constables of the watch, rather than apprentices, and their cry of 'clubs', although still linked to violence ('Beat them down!'), is primarily aimed at ending conflict rather than starting it anew. Still, the presence of a large gathering of violent young men onstage, together with the cultural association of clubs with riots instigated by working men, injects this opening scene with a palpable undercurrent of artisanal violence that amplifies, and arguably makes more dangerous, the more obvious threat of aristocratic violence that will erupt in the main plot.

In both *Coriolanus* and *Romeo and Juliet*, clubs appear onstage as props, not just as allusions in the dialogue. However, if we turn our attention to a very different tragedy—*Titus Andronicus*—we can examine how Shakespeare transforms the verbal resonances of the word 'clubs' to surprising dramatic effect. In the opening scene of Act 2 of *Titus*—a play rarely, if ever, discussed in terms of labour—we are introduced to Aaron and to Chiron and Demetrius, two sons of Tamora, the Queen of the Goths. Aaron comes upon the two brothers quarrelling over Titus' daughter Lavinia and exclaims: 'Clubs, clubs! These lovers will not keep the peace' (2.1.37). As the scene continues, Aaron intervenes in the brothers' quarrel, warning them against maintaining 'such a quarrel openly' (2.1.47), and eventually redirecting their violence towards Lavinia. Given this context, the phrase 'clubs, clubs', is, on the surface, a rather curious one: although Chiron and Demetrius prepare to fight before Aaron intervenes, they draw rapiers (not clubs), as appropriate to their elevated social position, and the phrase seems irrelevant to the ensuing exchange between Aaron and the brothers.

However, Aaron's interjection is far from insignificant. As a physical object, as we've seen, clubs were often associated with the collective violence performed (or feared to be performed) by Elizabethan apprentices and artisans. But the specific phrase 'clubs, clubs' had additional significance beyond the object to which it alludes: it was a popular street cry made to call forth apprentices in Shakespeare's London. The phrase is recounted in Holinshed's *Chronicles* (which in turn takes it from Edward Hall's *Chronicle* of 1548) in relation to the Evil May Day Riots of 1517, when groups of London servants and apprentices attacked foreigners. Hall records the cry of 'prentyses and clubbes' arising out of the 1517 riots, and Holinshed similarly describes 'the rising of prentices to the cry of "Clubs!" "Clubs"'.[32] Interestingly, despite the fact that the connection between this cry and apprentices was well established in popular discourse, the precise intent of the exclamation was often ambiguous. The cry could be deployed for two opposing purposes: either to preserve the peace or to rally the apprentices to fight—a discrepancy we saw at work in the opening scenes of *Coriolanus* and *Romeo and Juliet*.[33]

Aaron's line thus invokes a popular language that early modern playgoers would have readily associated with apprentice labour and with the violence with which it was often connected in the cultural imagination. But unlike *Coriolanus* or even *Romeo and Juliet*, this reference seems curiously out of place in this scene: no artisans or apprentices are present onstage, nor is the scene in question one of mob violence or organized revolt. What, then, might be the significance of Aaron's allusion to apprentices in this scene? One answer is that Aaron's seemingly odd hailing of the brothers as apprentices activates several themes that are important to the tragedy as a whole. In his entreaty to them, for instance, Aaron seeks to deflect the brothers' violence by appealing to forms of national and political solidarity. At first glance, Aaron's exasperation that 'these lovers will not keep the peace' seems to imply that his refrain of 'clubs, clubs' is an attempt at conciliation. However, the remainder of the scene, and Aaron's relationship with the two brothers during the rest of the play, complicates this reading. Instead of urging peace, Aaron goes on to incite the brothers to turn their anger outward, back to Lavinia herself, whom they will brutally rape and mutilate later in the act. As was true of the Evil May Day riots in 1517, London apprentice riots in the 1580s and 1590s were frequently directed at foreigners, who were blamed for taking skilled jobs away from English livery company members. But in *Titus* (first performed in 1594), it is Chiron, Demetrius, and Aaron himself who are the foreigners in Rome. Indeed, Roman authority seems dominant in the play, so much so that Tamora tries to co-opt it for her own purposes in the opening scene. As she declares in an attempt to gain favor with her Roman conquerors, 'Titus, I am incorporate in Rome, | A Roman now adopted happily' (1.1.459–60). Aaron takes a different approach, however. His cry of 'clubs, clubs' linguistically associates the brothers not with the Romans, but with apprentices fighting against a perceived foreign threat. In doing so, Aaron uses the language of apprentice rallies to fuel political revenge against the Romans. He essentially constructs an alternative narrative in which Chiron, Demetrius, and Aaron are 'insiders' fighting against the Roman 'outsiders'. And his strategy is successful: his ploy to redirect the brothers' violence results almost immediately in a change of plans. Moments after Aaron's exclamation,[34] Demetrius suggests the danger of intramural violence and the need to shift focus elsewhere when he asks Chiron: 'Are you so desperate grown to threat your friends?' (2.1.40). Instead of attacking each other, they will turn their violence on the Romans, and on Lavinia in particular.

Aaron's cry of 'clubs, clubs' also indirectly spurs the brothers to violence by highlighting their social vulnerability and desire for upward mobility. In discussing causes of apprentice riots in the period, Ian Archer notes: 'The loyalties of the artisans were essentially conditional, dependent on the rulers being sufficiently responsive to their demands to ensure their continuing obedience.'[35] The maintenance of order, that is, was in large part determined by apprentices' *perceptions* of injustice at the hands of authorities. Aaron's rallying cry thus may touch a nerve with the brothers, playing on their desire for social betterment, a desire shared by Aaron himself: in his opening monologue, he chastises himself to 'Away with slavish weeds and servile thoughts!' (2.1.18). The phrase 'clubs, clubs', therefore, can be seen as part of a much larger dramaturgical process in the play whereby the very nature of political, national, and social loyalties is challenged and reimagined. Aaron deploys the language of apprentice solidarity against immigrant workers and redirects it. His cry of 'clubs, clubs' conjures up images of the comradery established through artisanal labour and citizenship. However, by urging them to deflect their violence onto Lavinia, Aaron adopts that image of loyalty to manipulate Chiron and Demetrius' lust for his own political purposes of revenge. Aaron thus asks the audience to reimagine a simple fight between two brothers in terms of a collective brawl that repositions them in a narrative of political and national conflict, themes that the rest of the play will explore in bloody and complex detail.

This example demonstrates the powerful utility of figurative references to artisans and apprentices, even when that work is absent from Shakespeare's stage. In *Titus*, the phrase 'clubs, clubs!' enables Shakespeare to quickly draw on a popular language associated with artisanal violence and protests in order to develop his characters, themes, and plot. This brief phrase, in other words, consolidates an entire range of suggestive meanings (about craft workers, violence, social order, national identity, and the power of collective groups) and allows them to come into play for the audience all at once. We might think of this example of Shakespeare's 'working words' as a kind of dramaturgical shortcut of sorts, an effective tool for verbally acclimating the audience to specific contexts, perspectives, and even emotions. Even when he does not stage working characters or scenes of labour directly, then, Shakespeare draws on allusive references to work to shape the dramatic texture of his plays, including in places (such as the scene between Aaron, Chiron, and Demetrius in *Titus*) where we might least expect it. In the next two chapters, we will explore in more detail how Shakespeare uses indirect or figurative references to labour to animate his dramatic characters and scenes.

Shakespeare and Work. Michelle M. Dowd, Oxford University Press. © Michelle M. Dowd 2026.
DOI: 10.1093/9780191998096.003.0005

5

Working the Green World

As the discussion of the phrase 'clubs, clubs' in the previous chapter demonstrates, examining Shakespeare's verbal allusions to work can significantly shift our understanding of his plays, including plays such as *Titus Andronicus* that are rarely discussed in terms of labour. This chapter delves deeper into Shakespeare's metaphoric and expressive representations of work by turning attention to agricultural labour. This category of work, which includes farming, harvesting, and tending to livestock, among other tasks, is very rarely depicted on the early modern stage, either by Shakespeare or his contemporaries. Unlike Jacobean city comedies, which often stage the day-to-day work of urban shopkeepers and artisans, pastoral comedies from the late sixteenth and early seventeenth centuries usually refrain from directly representing rural labour and instead offer a more generalized, and often romanticized, picture of rural life. For Shakespeare, these scenes often comprise what has come to be known as 'green world' settings—a comedic respite from the problems of the everyday 'real' world to be found in the court or city. After providing an initial overview of agricultural work and how it was changing in the early modern period, this chapter will discuss the dramatic concept of the green world as it applies to Shakespeare's plays. Considering examples from a range of plays, including *As You Like It*, *The Winter's Tale*, and *The Tempest*, the chapter will suggest that while agricultural work may not be directly staged in Shakespeare's green worlds, it is nevertheless vividly present there via figurative language. Indeed, we will see that agricultural labour is often the necessary precondition for the structure and rhythm of these dramatic spaces. The chapter concludes with a longer examination of *Love's Labour's Lost*, a play that, despite its title, has rarely been discussed in terms of work. Reading *Love's Labour's Lost* as a green world play enables us to see how the temporal structure of this comedy is powerfully informed by Shakespeare's evocation of agrarian labour.

Agricultural Work in Shakespeare's England

The vast majority of people in Shakespeare's England lived not in major cities such as London, but in small towns and rural areas. Agricultural production and its related crafts were thus the primary focus of most English families throughout the period. Although certainly not all rural residents were themselves agricultural labourers, and significant regional differences altered the economic landscape in different parts of the country, historians have estimated that across the Tudor and Stuart period 'the labouring population probably formed about one quarter or one third of the entire population of the countryside'.[1] Some of these labourers worked in stock-farming, raising and tending to cattle, sheep, and other livestock. Others worked in arable farming, growing, tending to, and harvesting grain and other crops. The range of potential tasks was diverse and often quite demanding, requiring both physical strength and a range of other skills, such as the proper handling of tools. Typical jobs included threshing, ploughing, planting, weeding, mowing, shepherding, and carting. Like the servants and apprentices discussed in the previous two chapters, agrarian workers often started in their teens, gaining expertise by working either as annual or seasonal labourers. And they too experienced periods of precarity or unemployment, often leading to physical displacement.[2]

Agricultural work was seasonal, following the rhythms of climate and natural growth patterns. There was, then, a well-defined calendar of rural labour, especially labour in the fields tending to crops. Broadly speaking, there were four main periods of work, each connected to one of the seasons. Winter (the period between Michaelmas and Christmas) was the time for the sowing of grain, especially wheat and rye. Spring, from Christmas to Easter, saw the sowing of oats, barley, peas, and beans as well as weeding and other maintenance. The work of shearing and harvesting began in summer, lasting from Easter to Lammas Day (1 August; Figure 5.1), with the harvest continuing through to the

Figure 5.1 'Summer (Aestas)', from *The Seasons*. Engraving by Pieter van der Heyden after Pieter Bruegel the Elder (1570). Courtesy of the Metropolitan Museum of Art.

autumn (from Lammas back to Michaelmas).[3] Printed calendars and illustrations linking various types of agricultural work to each month and season of the year were popular textual reminders of these temporal connections. That tradition dates back to the medieval period, where the 'labours of the months'—a series of 'conventional images of workers engaged in seasonally appropriate activities'—was a 'familiar motif in public buildings and books of hours'.[4] In Shakespeare's England, one of the most popular texts in this tradition was Thomas Tusser's *Five Hundred Points of Good Husbandry*, first published in 1557 as *A Hundreth Good Points of Husbandrie* and expanded in 1580. As a testament to its popularity, the text went through twenty-three editions between 1557 and 1638.[5] Tusser's text is written in verse and organized in a month-by-month format. The rhyming verses remind readers of the labours connected to each season of the year. For instance, here is one of the opening stanzas of the section on 'October's Husbandry':

> Greene rye in September when timely thou hast,
> October for wheat sowing calleth as fast.
> If weather will suffer, this counsel I give,
> Leave sowing of wheat before Hallowmas eve.[6]

Tusser's compact verses connect agricultural labours to a specific seasonal time frame, offering farmers a practical mnemonic, but also providing general readers with a clear sense of the seasonality of agrarian work.

Despite many continuities in work patterns and seasonal rhythms that extended from the Middle Ages through Shakespeare's lifetime, changes in rural labour during the sixteenth century significantly affected how and what work was performed and how that labour was culturally understood. As we've seen, one of the most profound of these changes was the rapid growth of the English population over the course of the sixteenth and early seventeenth centuries. As a result, the 'prices of basic commodities soared', creating a 'pressing need for increased agricultural productivity'.[7] To meet this new demand, farmers turned to a variety of strategies, including cultivating land that had previously been unused (or only lightly used) and introducing new crops, fertilizers, and equipment to improve productivity. The Statute of Artificers, discussed in Chapter 1, was developed in part to address deficiencies in agricultural production in order to feed England's growing population. The Statute attempted to meet this goal by restricting the mobility of rural workers through long-term contracts and requiring able-bodied workers to assist with farming, especially during harvest time. Over time, both the ownership and the occupancy of rural lands became concentrated in fewer and fewer hands. Not surprisingly, while landowners stood to do fairly well economically, tenant farmers—those who rented lands from wealthier owners—did not enjoy such rosy prospects.[8]

The increasing demand to produce more food to feed a rapidly growing population gave rise to a host of new texts that emphasized farming techniques and strategies for improving the land to increase yields. These 'husbandry' manuals, including Tusser's extremely popular

Five Hundred Points of Good Husbandry, emphasized that 'without cultivation, the Elizabethan economy could not survive and neither could its subjects'. These texts marked a significant shift in cultural attitudes towards farming and agricultural production, as they tended to 'valorize expectations of profit' as part of a new 'moral discourse of social relations', given the demographic realities of sixteenth-century English life.[9] Discourses of agricultural 'improvement', in other words, were increasingly framed in terms of business and profit, where land was viewed as a productive resource rather than simply a place to live.[10] Tusser's verse treatise was one of the most important texts on good farm management in the period, but, as we will see, Shakespeare's plays also participated in this ongoing conversation about the daily routines and larger functions of agrarian labour.

The increased emphasis on agricultural improvement over the course of the sixteenth century was in part responsible for one of the most significant (and controversial) developments in the period: enclosure. In basic terms, enclosure referred to the practice by which lands were hedged or fenced in to put an end to common grazing rights. Arable land and open fields worked by tenants were thus enclosed and converted into pasture. Enclosure was certainly not unique to the early modern period, as much land in England had been enclosed in the late Middle Ages. However, enclosure practices occurred at a rapid pace in the sixteenth and seventeenth centuries, which further undermined the positions of tenant farmers at the expense of wealthier landowners.[11] The effects of enclosure were multiple and complex, but it heralded a new era of work and landownership that 'extended the rights of individuals over those of a community', and, as a result, enclosure 'became the symbolic battleground between custom and improvement'.[12]

These important changes to agrarian labour and landownership in the period form a vital backdrop for reading Shakespeare's plays, as his audiences would have been well versed in many of the particulars of rural working life and with the controversies surrounding enclosure and other related practices. Indeed, we see Shakespeare directly alluding to the enclosure debate in his characterization of Jack Cade and his group of rebels in *2 Henry VI*, a play discussed in more detail in Chapter 4. Speaking to his fellow artisans and rebels-in-arms, Cade several times repeats his rallying cry that 'All the realm shall be in common' (4.2.70, and again at 4.7.17: 'all things shall be in common'). Cade touches here on the profound dissatisfaction faced by many tenant farmers who protested enclosure, viewed as a land-grab by the wealthy. His hopeful promise to make lands common again echoes and responds implicitly to the petitioners depicted in the first act of the play, one of whom protests 'Against the Duke of Suffolk for enclosing the commons of Melford' (1.3.22–3). And in his final scene, Cade dies at the hands of Alexander Iden, a landowning gentleman (whom Cade refers to as 'the lord of the soil' [4.9.24]) who has enclosed his private garden with a brick wall.[13] Shakespeare represents Cade as in the wrong for scaling the wall and trespassing on Iden's lands, but the play nevertheless leaves open broader questions about enclosure, rightful land stewardship, and the plight of agrarian workers. In *2 Henry VI*, Shakespeare brings enclosure practices directly into the dialogue as an important context for the social unrest he stages. As we will see, agrarian labour and its vital social contexts often form a more subtle, yet no less vital, component of other plays in Shakespeare's oeuvre. This is especially true of his comedies and in his depiction of the green world, to which we now turn.

Shakespeare and the Green World

When considering Shakespeare's romantic and pastoral comedies, scholars have often turned to the concept of the green world as a useful frame of analysis. The idea of the green world in modern criticism dates back to the work of Northrop Frye, who defined the green world as a fictional world within comedy that represents a fertile, even dreamlike space that stands as a 'symbol of natural society' in direct contrast to the normal world from which most of the play's characters begin and to which they typically return at the comedy's conclusion.[14] According to Frye, the green world is closely connected with seasonality, and it 'charges the comedies with the symbolism of the victory of summer over winter'.[15] The 'rhythmic movement from normal world to green world and back again' becomes a defining structural feature that Frye asserts is to be found in different forms in all of Shakespeare's comedies.[16] As Frye and numerous later critics have suggested, Shakespeare's comedies depend on the creation of this (physical and metaphorical) space of leisure or escape to prepare for the resolution of dramatic conflict—enabling characters (for instance) to grow and learn before they return to the day-to-day life of the real world. We can think of the Forest of Arden in *As You Like It* and the woods outside Athens in *A Midsummer Night's Dream* as classic examples of such green world spaces.

Despite their typically rural settings and seasonal links to pastoral agriculture, Shakespeare's green worlds have often been viewed as largely free of labour, rather than as places where agrarian work is highlighted. As Raymond Williams argues in *The Country and the City*, labour and poverty are often erased from literary representations of the pastoral and rural life, including the romanticized rural spaces of the Shakespearian green world. In his analysis of country house poems by Ben Jonson, Thomas Carew, and others, for instance, Williams traces a 'magical extraction of the curse of labour' that is achieved 'by a simple extraction of the existence of labourers'. The 'actual men and women' who perform agriculture work are not present in these literary representations; instead, their 'work is all done for them by a natural order'.[17] Similarly, Adam Zucker, writing of the development of the green world motif through Shakespeare and into later Caroline comedies, argues that in early seventeenth-century plays the green world provides 'a familiar vision of a labor-less London'.[18] As a result, Shakespeare's green worlds are typically read as spaces that stand in opposition to labour, and even as spaces from which labour has been purposely erased.

But acknowledging that the green world is often structurally positioned in opposition to labour (as a space of leisure or retreat) is not the same as arguing that labour is entirely absent from these plays. Writers of the period certainly viewed pastoral literature as fully compatible with the everyday labour of rural life.[19] And narrow definitions of literary modes such as pastoral can often miss the broader contexts within with Shakespeare was writing. Regardless of their direct connection to classical models of pastoral, in other words, Shakespeare's comedies engage in multiple, meaningful ways with the world of agrarian production.[20] Indeed, when we look more closely at Shakespeare's comedies, we find that labour remains resiliently *present* in the green world in ways we haven't fully accounted for. Even if the green world is often represented as a space of leisure rather than labour, attending to the dramatic language that Shakespeare uses to create and sustain the illusion of the green world reveals that work—and specifically the rhythmic patterns of rural labour—is an important precondition that enables the green world to come into being in the first place. In many of his comedies, the structural rhythms of the green world are developed and sustained through images of agrarian work.

To be sure, what we find in the plays is usually not a realistic recognition of the hardships of rural life: Shakespeare instead frequently depicts a romanticized understanding of seasonality. Nevertheless, that seasonality is directly indebted to agrarian labour. The calendar of agricultural work so carefully set forth in month-by-month fashion by Tusser and other writers created a fundamental rhythm of everyday life that informed how people both worked and played.[21] Working the land imposed a kind of temporal order on human activities and enabled humans in turn to exert control over the natural world.[22] Shakespeare made use of these temporal structures to provide dramatic order in his plays that feature green world settings of leisure and wildness. The seasonality of agricultural work, in other words, provides a useful dramatic structure for Shakespeare: it enables him to impose order on the romantic trajectory of his comedies, and on the green worlds that he stages. Rather than erasing labour, Shakespeare constructs his green worlds in and through figurative images of rural work.

Agrarian Work in Shakespeare's Comedies

Although some earlier readers of Shakespeare claimed that he made only minimal use of agricultural language, we can see quite clearly when we turn to the plays themselves that this is not the case.[23] Through his upbringing in Stratford, Shakespeare was well acquainted with rural life and perhaps as a result he, arguably more than other playwrights of his era, 'attends to cultivation as a discourse of value' in his plays.[24] Throughout his career, even when writing from the urban world of London, Shakespeare remained invested in images of agricultural labour. For instance, he often includes offhand references to the work of agrarian husbandry, such as ploughing, within an exchange of dialogue. One example appears in *1 Henry IV*, when Davy asks Shallow if they should 'sow the headland with wheat' (5.1.12). Here, Shakespeare directly references what was known as the strip-field system, in which a team of animals would plough a strip of land, but leave a bit (the headland) at each end of the long field on which the team would turn and rest. At other moments, Shakespeare takes specific allusions to agrarian labour and makes them the primary vehicle of his poetic tenor. For instance, Shakespeare again calls up the strip-field system in the final act of *As You Like It*, in the song 'It was a lover and his lass':

> Between the acres of the rye,
>   With a hey, and a ho, and a hey-nonny-no,
> These pretty country folks would lie,
>   In spring-time, the only pretty ring-time,
> When birds do sing, hey ding-a-ding ding,
>   Sweet lovers love the spring. (5.3.21–6)

As Robert Spier and Donald Anderson explain, 'the long strip-fields were separated by unplowed strips or ridges, at right angles to the headlands'. In the song, these 'unplowed strips between fields of rye' become the 'trysting places of lovers in the spring'.[25] Agricultural work here provides the poetic foundation necessary for pastoral romantic love to develop and flourish.

Indeed, *As You Like It* is a great example of a comedy that deploys images of agrarian labour to construct its traditional green world setting. In the Forest of Arden, where most of the play's action takes place following the opening scenes at court, Duke Senior and his lords live in voluntary exile and 'fleet the time carelessly, as they did in the golden world' (1.1.113). However, the play makes it clear that the green world can only exist as a carefree 'golden world' because hard work has paved the way for it. As we saw in Chapter 3, the loyal servant Adam helps his master Orlando flee to Arden by giving him 'five hundred crowns' from his 'youthful wages' (2.3.39, 68). Adam's labour thus directly enables Orlando's fanciful green world escapades. Once in Arden, we also see traces of the rural work and hard economic conditions that literary pastoral often tends to elide. Rosalind and Celia meet the shepherd Corin in the forest, who alludes to some of the hardships brought about by enclosure.[26] He bemoans his poor financial circumstances, explaining that he cannot help the travellers because: 'I am shepherd to another man, | And do not shear the fleeces that I graze' (2.4.77–8). The absent landowner is of a 'churlish disposition', with little care for his own 'flock and pasture', which he has put up for sale (79, 87). Corin's situation might well resonate with audience members familiar with the controversies surrounding enclosure, and it highlights the labour that Corin has individually performed to maintain the land and livestock. At the same time, the play resolves Corin's situation with a comically rapid and expedient fix in the form of Rosalind's offer to give Corin the money so that he can buy the 'cottage, pasture and the flock' outright (91). Rosalind's rank and wealth perform a kind of *deus ex machina* function, magically transforming Corin's financial position and sidelining the concerns about poverty provoked by enclosure. This is a highly romanticized rendering of rural labour, to be sure, one that seems to clear the way for romantic rather than economic relationships to thrive.

And yet, even in the idyllic world of Arden, which seems more focused on leisure than on labour, Shakespeare gives voice to rural work through allusions and figurative language that often serve to underscore the rhythms of romantic love. The lovesick Silvius, for instance, tells his beloved Phoebe of his unrequited feelings by invoking the patterns of the harvest:

> So holy and so perfect is my love,
> And I in such a poverty of grace,
> That I shall think it a most plenteous crop
> To glean the broken ears after the man
> That the main harvest reaps. (3.5.100–4).

Silvius describes his desire for Phoebe as a process of harvesting, divided into the 'main' harvest and the subsidiary one of gathering the 'broken ears', an image that suggests the possibility of narrative trajectory and at least partial fulfilment. Even Touchstone, in his mocking ridicule of the bad poetry Orlando has written to Rosalind, draws upon a similar image to describe romantic love: 'They that reap must sheaf and bind, | Then to cart with Rosalind' (3.2.105–6). In both instances, as in the song 'It was a lover and his lass', the harvest imagery conjures up a temporal pattern that gently imposes order on the chaotic green world activities of the lovers: just as planting will eventually lead to harvest, so too will lovers eventually find their communion.

While *As You Like It*'s pastoral setting makes it especially well suited to this kind of agricultural imagery, we find similar allusions in several other green world comedies where rural labour is a less obvious point of reference. In *A Midsummer Night's Dream*, for instance, the lovers flee to the woods outside Athens, where most of the play's action takes place. Lysander, having been newly anointed with the juice of a magical flower by Robin, shifts the focus of his love from Hermia to Helena. Telling Helena of his new-found feelings for her, he says:

> The will of man is by his reason swayed,
> And reason says you are the worthier maid.
> Things growing are not ripe until their season,
> So I, being young, till now ripe not to reason. (2.2.121–4)

As in *As You Like It*, Lysander's declaration articulates the maturation of desire in terms of the seasonal pattern of ripening and harvesting crops. The rhythms of agrarian labour provide the narrative template that supports Lysander's new romantic pronouncement, offering a logical rationale for his otherwise unexplainable change of heart. In this way, the temporality inherent to agricultural labour helps counter the romantic chaos of the green world.

Shakespeare deploys a similar metaphor linking the harvest to romantic maturity in *Twelfth Night*, a play in which the green world setting of Illyria is decidedly courtly rather than rural in focus. Speaking with Viola, disguised as Cesario, Olivia continues to reject Orsino's protestations of love and instead turns the focus of her desire to his page. After hearing the clock strike, she tells Viola/Cesario:

> The clock upbraids me with the waste of time.
> Be not afraid, good youth, I will not have you;
> And yet when wit and youth is come to harvest
> Your wife is like to reap a proper man. (3.1.129–32)

Olivia shifts quickly from the idea of wasting time to the image of the harvest, when 'wit and youth' will come to maturity and romantic love can be properly realized. The labour of reaping the harvest offers a way to gauge the passing of time, as well as a measure of the 'proper' spending of time rather than the wasting of it. But it also serves as a figurative marker of appropriate behaviour and development, a process whereby Viola/Cesario will one day become a 'proper man' who will reach romantic maturity. In all of these examples, the imagery of agrarian labour creates a sense of progression and dramatic order that helps Shakespeare shape the trajectory of his green world comedies.

Shakespeare would return to the green world and to images of agricultural work in his late tragicomedies, particularly in *The Tempest* and *The Winter's Tale*. Although these plays differ from his earlier romantic comedies due to their more serious tone and subject matter, the green world remains a powerful thematic space in which Shakespeare can depict the growth and transformation of his characters. And he does this both through direct onstage examples of rural labour and also, more extensively, through his settings, allusions, and verbal imagery. We will return to *The Tempest* and *The Winter's Tale* and examine them in more detail in Chapter 6, but for now we can observe how Shakespeare uses agrarian images in these late plays to highlight the trajectory of romantic love, as he did in his earlier comedies. In *The Tempest*, the play's unnamed island and central locale serves as a green world setting, an otherworldly and at times threatening place where Antonio, Alonso, and the other European lords find themselves shipwrecked, yet magically preserved from harm. When Alonso's son Ferdinand falls in love with Prospero's daughter Miranda, Prospero stages a masque, an elaborate theatrical entertainment, to celebrate their engagement. The masque offers a respite from the political scheming and revenge plots going on elsewhere in the play, as the entertainment transports viewers to a mythological world of rural abundance. During the masque, Ceres, the Roman goddess of agriculture and fertility, appears and blesses the betrothed couple by describing a successful cycle of agricultural work in which labour brings harvest (followed by rest) and barns and storehouses ('garners') are full of grain (4.1.111).[27] Ceres' speech in *The Tempest* connects the process of proper development and fulfilment of heterosexual love with the seasonal rhythms of rural labour, providing a degree of order to what has otherwise been a magically chaotic world, much like the woods outside Athens in *A Midsummer Night's Dream*.

In *The Winter's Tale*, Shakespeare devotes the entirety of Act 4, scene 4—one of the longest scenes in any of Shakespeare's plays—to a pastoral setting, featuring a sheep-shearing festival. Shakespeare greatly expanded on this scene from his primary source, Robert Greene's *Pandosto*, giving it heightened focus in his late tragicomedy. England's major industry in the early seventeenth century when the play was written was the wool trade, making the tending of sheep a key component of agrarian labour. Sheep-shearing was one of the major agricultural tasks that occurred in summer, typically June, and its importance to the rural economy was marked by formal celebrations and feasts.[28] In *The Winter's Tale*, the sheep-shearing festival serves as the backdrop for the announcement of Florizel and Perdita's love, the catalyst that will return them to Sicily in the next act and lead ultimately to reconciliation with Leontes and a new marital union. The pastoral setting of Bohemia provides another green world locale where love can be both announced and tested, in this case by the angry intervention of Florizel's father Polixenes, who rejects the union, not knowing Perdita's true noble identity. The scene certainly romanticizes its rural setting, highlighting festive rituals and (as we'll see in the next chapter) commercial activity rather than the details of rural work. But the underlying context and allusive setting is nevertheless highly significant: the seasonal rhythms of agrarian labour provide a dramatic structure for tracing the development and maturation of romantic love. The scene marks a transition from the first part of the play and its final resolution, both set at the court in Sicily. The movement of the plot from tragedy and towards reconciliation, in other words, is made possible through this extended scene of rural labour and ritual.[29]

Rural labour is thus in many ways intrinsic to the structure of the green world not only in Shakespeare's earlier romantic comedies, but also in his later tragicomedies. Even though we do not usually see actors performing the physical tasks of agricultural work onstage in these plays, the rhythmic structures of seasonal work patterns inflect Shakespeare's poetry, plotting, and character development in significant ways, offering a kind of counterpoint to his green world settings, which are necessarily chaotic, filled as they are with magic, mistaken identities, and even (especially in the late plays) threats of violence. In the final section of this chapter, we shift focus back to one of Shakespeare's earlier romantic comedies that has often been left out of discussions of both the green world and labour. In doing so, we'll see how agricultural labour helps shape Shakespeare's comedic dramaturgy in surprising, yet meaningful ways.

Finding Labour in *Love's Labour's Lost*

Despite its title, *Love's Labour's Lost* (1594–5) is a play that is rarely (if ever) discussed in terms of labour. As Louis Montrose has noted, almost all of the fictional action of the play is generated 'by characters at play' rather than at work, resulting in a courtly comedy that is an 'ornate and stylized artifact with a surface resemblance to the court plays of [John] Lyly'.[30] The play's aristocratic romantic plot makes it even more of an 'elite' comedy than plays such as *A Midsummer Night's Dream* or *The Comedy of Errors* from around the same period. The King of Navarre's park serves as a particularly elite version of the green world space, with the abrupt call back to reality by the news of the death of the King of France at the end of the play marking the somewhat untidy social reintegration of the comedy's romantic protagonists. And certainly, work in the form of stage business (e.g. carrying logs, à la *The Tempest*) or direct representation (e.g. *Midsummer*'s mechanicals) is absent from this highly stylized and linguistically expressive play.[31] And yet, we can find a great deal of work in *Love's Labour's Lost* if we know where to look for it. Indeed, it is precisely in the play's lyrical wordplay that we can see the subtle yet significant workings of rural labour patterns and how they shape the play's temporal movements.

The play's opening scene announces the importance of time to this comedy, as Navarre discusses with his lords his planned edict to make his kingdom 'the wonder of the world' through a three-year period of academic retreat and study (1.1.12). In Navarre's opening lines, he champions fame at the expense of 'cormorant devouring time' (4) and pronounces that their collective endeavours will 'bate his scythe's keen edge' (6). The familiar image of death as a reaper establishes one temporal system, governed by both mortality and the rhythms of agricultural labour (or rather mortality via the rhythms of such labour). Navarre pointedly refutes this temporal order, offering instead a three-year interim of contemplative life that, despite its finite duration, will make him and his lords 'heirs of all eternity' (7) through everlasting renown. Indeed, by reiterating the phrase 'three years' eight separate times in this opening scene, Navarre and his lords seem eager to codify and fix this concrete duration of time in the face of the more amorphous rhythms of death-as-harvester. By evoking and then denouncing a seasonal flux rooted in agricultural labour patterns, the opening scene sets up a jesting mismatch between two models of time.

The comedic payoffs of this disjunction are soon apparent. Although Longueville and Dumaine quickly sign on to Navarre's plan, Biron raises objections to the proposed stipulations that extend beyond the basic promise to study with Navarre and remain at court for three years:

> But there are other strict observances,
> As not to see a woman in that term,
> Which I hope well is not enrollèd there;
> And one day in a week to touch no food,
> And but one meal on every day beside,
> The which I hope is not enrollèd there;
> And then to sleep but three hours in the night,
> And not be seen to wink of all the day
> When I was wont to think no harm all night,
> And make a dark night too of half the day,
> Which I hope well is not enrollèd there.
> Oh, these are barren tasks, too hard to keep—
> Not to see ladies, study, fast, not sleep. (36–48)

Biron specifically questions the regimented temporality of Navarre's proposal, broken down into days and hours restricted to certain purposes. Notably, he decries the limits on food, sleep, play, and romantic love as 'barren tasks', picking up Navarre's earlier agricultural metaphor to argue that this attempt at human-imposed order on natural cycles is futile because it is opposed to a kind of comic fecundity. Biron returns to the more amorphous seasonal temporality rejected by Navarre in his opening speech, but he does not go so far as to champion the rhythms of the scythe invoked earlier. Although the idea of barrenness implies the absence of harvest and the labour it requires, Biron does not make that specific comparison in his critique of the King's proposed 'barren tasks'. At this early point in the play, Biron seems to prefer the philosophical model offered by the festive rather than the workaday rhythms of rural life. As we will see, however, the opposition between barrenness and harvesting will be explicitly invoked later in the play—by none other than Biron himself.

In the meantime, the play's opening scene continues to emphasize how Navarre and his lords are out of sync with the seasonal rhythms of agricultural production. Mocking Biron's long-winded critique of Navarre's plan, the lords respond by again invoking a seasonal temporality:

> KING How well he's read, to reason against reading!
> DUMAINE Proceeded well, to stop all good proceeding.
> LONGUEVILLE He weeds the corn and still lets grow the weeding.
> BIRON The spring is near when green geese are a-breeding.
> DUMAINE How follows that?
> BIRON Fit in his place and time.
> DUMAINE In reason nothing.
> BIRON Something, then, in rhyme.
> KING Biron is like an envious sneaping frost,
> That bites the first-born infants of the spring. (94–101)

Biron goes on to retort that he prefers to enjoy 'each thing that in season grows' (107). Longueville's comments about Biron's 'weeding' link his rhetorical manoeuvring to the process of tending to crops, yet chastise him for doing a poor job of it.[32] Biron's response offers what he sees as a more appropriate seasonal model; green geese feed on grass, not corn (i.e. wheat) and lay eggs between February and May.[33] Biron refutes Longueville's critique by correcting his rural image set: he predicts that the lords will themselves be seeking mates soon, and he insists on the proper seasonal metaphor—'fit in his place and time'—to make his case. Here, then, Biron introduces a notion of natural fertility and growth based on the seasonal patterns of rural agricultural production: growing, breeding, weeding, and ultimately harvesting. These seasonal labour patterns invoke a world of fecundity and mortality that is at odds with Navarre's almost legalistic focus on the precise term of three years' duration throughout the scene.[34] This exchange helps establish the male protagonists as temporally out of sync with the rhythms of festive comedy, and heteronormative fertility more specifically. A different temporal awareness will become necessary by the end of the play.

If *Love's Labour's Lost* opens with Navarre's alternative model of plotting time, that plan is quickly dispensed with when the Princess and her ladies enter the park. And although Biron may be the shrewdest of the quartet in terms of noting the unseasonal attitudes of the lords in the opening scene, he too ultimately needs to accept the rhythms of rural labour that are hinted at early in the comedy. In the discovery scene, in which each of the men confesses his love and is secretly overheard by the others, Biron describes his love-sick companions as '[m]ore sacks to the mill' (4.3.78) and contrasts the pursuit of love to other 'slow arts' that 'finding barren practisers, | Scarce show a harvest of their heavy toil' (300–2). Here Biron makes good on the metaphor of barrenness implicit in his earlier critiques by explicitly contrasting such sterility with the hard work of growing and bringing in a crop. Love, he proposes, is a pursuit in which labour leads to generation in both external effect (the harvest itself) and self-awareness (transforming 'barren practisers' into more productive citizens). In his final charge to the men at the scene's conclusion, Biron urges them on by saying: 'Sowed cockle reaped no corn' (359). In other words, the crop (wheat, or 'corn') cannot be harvested where weeds ('cockle') have been sown.[35] Returning full-circle to Longueville's earlier complaint about Biron letting weeds grow despite his labour, Biron now argues that labour, not festivity alone, is required to enable the promise of romantic fulfilment. But the imagery that runs through these exchanges makes it clear that it is not simply 'labour' in a generalized sense, but the quotidian patterns of rural farming that lie behind this comic trajectory. And what might such imagery be doing in this decidedly aristocratic play? In *Love's Labour's Lost*, this workaday imagery, based in the decidedly non-elite world of agrarian life and labour, has a particular use-value: it enables Shakespeare to explore and reframe the mechanisms of comedic temporality.

The news of the King of France's death in the play's final scene draws this comedy to its unexpected and unusual conclusion. Instead of agreeing to the men's offers of love, the Princess responds to the tragic news by proposing a one-year hiatus while she mourns for her father, a decision that further delays romantic fulfilment rather than resolving it. But it also recalls Navarre's flouting of death's scythe in his opening monologue; mortality cannot be delayed or put at bay simply by withdrawing from the ebb and flow of nature's temporal progression. The conclusion of this comedy, vexed as it is, requires the lords to at last come to a proper understanding of time. Biron seems to get at the heart of the matter when he tells the ladies, 'For your fair sakes have we neglected time' (5.2.747), reminding us of the lords' adversarial approach to seasonal time earlier in the play. Indeed, the final series of exchanges between the lovers and the concluding pair of songs make it clear that acceptance of temporal patterns based in the rhythms of an agrarian calendar is necessary to comic conclusion, however deferred. When the Princess (now Queen) of France sets forth the required twelve-month postponement that concludes the play, she reimagines the lords' proposed three-year sequestration in quite different terms that embrace rather than deny seasonality. She instructs them to go to 'some forlorn and naked hermitage', but to stay there 'until the twelve celestial signs | Have brought about the annual reckoning.' She will wait to see whether 'frosts and fasts ... | Nip not the gaudy blossoms of your love' (787–94). Emphasizing a retreat that is still attuned to seasonal change, she sets up the context for the comedy's closing songs.

In the two songs that conclude the play, Shakespeare stages a conventional debate between spring ('When daisies pied and violets blue') and winter ('When icicles hang by the wall'). In these songs, more explicit images of agricultural and domestic labour—shepherding, gathering wood and milk, cooking, and ploughing—underwrite the seasonal debate and suggest a pattern of growth and death, wooing and marriage that extends and helps to clarify the Queen's pronouncement. Here is the concluding stanza of Spring's song:

> When shepherds pipe on oaten straws,
>   And merry larks are ploughmen's clocks;
> When turtles tread, and rooks and daws,
>   And maidens bleach their summer smocks,
> The cuckoo then on every tree
> Mocks married men, for thus sings he:
>   Cuckoo!
> Cuckoo, cuckoo—O word of fear,
> Unpleasing to a married ear. (888–96)

And here is the opening stanza of Winter's response:

> When icicles hang by the wall,
>   And Dick the shepherd blows his nail,

And Tom bears logs into the hall,
  And milk comes frozen home in pail;
When blood is nipped, and ways be foul,
Then nightly sings the staring owl:
Tu-whit, tu-whoo!—a merry note,
While greasy Joan doth keel the pot. (897–904)

This is not an 'either/or' debate, but rather an expression of the cyclical nature of the seasons that is punctuated by forms of everyday labour, perhaps most directly in Spring's observation that 'merry larks are ploughmen's clocks'. In this image, agricultural work both follows and creates a temporal rhythm that takes the place of the mechanical clock, an image that Shakespeare also uses to striking effect in sonnet 12. In that poem, Shakespeare establishes a similar contrast between agricultural time and clock time by juxtaposing the 'clock that tells the time' of the opening line with 'time's scythe' of the penultimate line. In doing so, Shakespeare holds in tension 'the ancient image of death derived from the manual labor of the harvest time' with the precise, mechanical time of the clock.[36] As in sonnet 12, images of agrarian labour in *Love's Labour's Lost*'s final songs presuppose an alternative model of telling time. Shakespeare is certainly romanticizing that temporal model here, but it is nevertheless poetically instrumental because it establishes a counter-narrative to the artificial, anti-fertile retreat envisioned by the lords in the opening scene. As Montrose notes, '[t]he songs wed play to work, love to labor, within the larger cyclical rhythms of a human community that is harmoniously wed to nature.'[37] The images of rural labour in these final songs function similarly to the masque in *The Tempest*, offering a temporal respite from the 'real' world of politics and human loss while also instilling the often-haphazard trajectory of the play's romantic plots with a degree of order connected to agricultural seasonality.

The comedic structure of *Love's Labour's Lost* is thus shaped in subtle, yet significant ways by a poetics of agricultural labour. The deferred, yet hoped-for resolution to this comedy requires a return to proper seasonality and an acceptance of change and mortality. We might think of this as a return to a kind of 'fertile' time that, metaphorically at least, can be enacted only through labour. The metaphoric appeal to the more populist world of agrarian labour affords not only a pathway to fertility, but also a narrative of imposed order, in contrast to the leisure and idleness often associated with the green world and festive comedy.[38] In this, then, perhaps the most 'elite' of Shakespearian comedies, we find that the decidedly non-elite activities of ploughing, weeding, and harvesting are surprisingly integral to the play's dramatic structure. Everyday forms of labour thus influence Shakespeare's comedy in ways that suggest a vital interconnection between the material conditions of labour and Shakespeare's dramatic aesthetic—two subjects that have often been separated, but that are ripe (pun intended) for reintegration.

Love's Labour's Lost is not a traditional green world comedy, nor a play usually considered in terms of labour. And yet, careful analysis of Shakespeare's language throughout this comedy reveals a consistent thread of imagery related to agricultural labour that helps establish the romantic and festive world of the play before its abrupt return to the 'real' world of politics in the final scene. As we've seen throughout this chapter, Shakespeare's green world plays—whether more typical examples of the genre, such as *As You Like It*, or variations on the traditional structure, such as *The Winter's Tale* and *Love's Labour's Lost*—incorporate a poetics of rural labour that may not always manifest in direct, onstage action, but instead constitutes an important figurative grounding for Shakespeare's characters and imaginative worlds. It is also crucial to the underlying comedic structure and formal rhythms of these plays. Labour in the green world may be elusive, it may be romanticized, and it may at times be downplayed in favour of leisure, but it is nevertheless powerfully present. In the next chapter, we will continue our investigation of Shakespeare's figurative use of agricultural work, but we will shift focus to the relationship between more traditional forms of rural labour and the emerging types of work necessitated by England's growing mercantile economy.

Shakespeare and Work. Michelle M. Dowd, Oxford University Press. © Michelle M. Dowd 2026.
DOI: 10.1093/9780191998096.003.0006

6

Going to Market

In the previous chapter, we examined how Shakespeare makes use of images drawn from the world of agricultural labour to establish the temporal rhythms of his green world comedies. Although rural work itself is largely absent from the stage, there is nevertheless a poetics of rural labour that powerfully shapes Shakespeare's dramatic worlds and characters in plays such as *As You Like It* and *Love's Labour's Lost*. This final chapter continues to focus on agricultural work as it manifests not directly through dramatic action, but indirectly through figurative language and allusion. However, we will look beyond the green world to explore the connection between agricultural labour, a traditional mainstay of the English economy, and newer forms of commercial work that developed during the country's gradual transition to capitalism. These two broad kinds of work existed uneasily together, as many people in Shakespeare's day were concerned about the ethical implications of mercantile labour and commercial profits as they pertained to traditional understandings of 'honest' work. The chapter begins with an overview of the new forms of work necessitated by England's growing capitalist economy, including venture capitalism, overseas trade, and novel forms of investment and commercial enterprise. It then considers a range of plays that bring together mercantile and agricultural labour in unexpected ways, including *The Merchant of Venice*, *Measure for Measure*, *The Merry Wives of Windsor*, and *Macbeth*, while also continuing the discussion of *The Winter's Tale* and *The Tempest* begun in the previous chapter. Through this analysis, this chapter reveals how Shakespeare stages the tensions between more traditional forms of agrarian labour and the rising world of commercial work. As we will see, in many of his plays Shakespeare deploys images of agricultural labour to mitigate concerns about and even at times lend credibility to newer forms of less tangible, market-based work.

Mercantile Labour and Trade in Shakespeare's England

The sixteenth and seventeenth centuries in England witnessed several large-scale socio-economic developments that influenced how people worked and to what ends. Shakespeare's England saw a substantial increase in trade and consumerism as English families became more dependent on goods produced outside the home. Beginning around 1550, England experienced a 'very rapid growth of trade',[1] and by the turn of the century, the number of imported goods had risen dramatically, due to both an increase in England's purchasing power and its growth as a 'commercial and colonial power, which brought much lower prices for some products'.[2] This new economic reality created a need for new kinds of work. In addition to the general shift within England's domestic economy from subsistence to commercial farming practices and an increased dependence upon goods purchased outside the home, the significant growth in England's imports also required an increase in mercantile activity to fulfil the country's demand for foreign goods. Overseas trading became not only a necessity, but also a lucrative line of work for many middling and elite Englishmen, with many members of the gentry, for instance, turning to foreign trade and investment to build the wealth required to maintain their family fortunes and estates. By the beginning of the seventeenth century, foreign trade held out the promise of a much greater return on investment than did domestic landholdings. Indeed, highly successful merchants were often able to earn enough wealth through trade that they could purchase the lands and titles traditionally reserved for those of more elite status.[3]

One change related to this new focus on overseas trade was the development of joint-stock companies. We saw in Chapter 1 that Elizabethan theatre companies were typically organized according to the joint-stock model of profit- and cost-sharing. Similarly, as merchants sought out ventures further and further away from England, they needed larger outlays of capital to finance these voyages. Joint-stock companies arose as a way for a group of traders to facilitate collective investments so as to share both risks and costs.[4] As L. C. Knights notes, 'The formation of joint-stock companies provided an opportunity for anyone with capital to invest, and from 1600 the sale of shares became increasingly common.'[5] One of the most profitable of these new companies was the East India Company. Incorporated in 1600, the Company offered 'consistent profits of 100 percent (and a return of up to 300 percent with many of its early voyages)'.[6] The foreign trade supported by the East India and other joint stock companies helped English colonialization become a fully commercialized endeavour. Through the development of trade routes both to the east and the west, English merchants sought out novel and highly lucrative sources of profits through commerce and the development of colonies. Indeed, the rise of imported luxury goods in the period was increasingly linked to the colonial economy. Consumer products such as tobacco, sugar, and coffee are some of the best known of these early colonial commodities, all of which 'required vast amounts of heavy labour, leading to the development of plantation economies' in the Caribbean and elsewhere.[7]

The growing imperatives of a market-based culture led many middling and wealthy landowners to 'embrace the new world of commerce' rather than focus their energies on more conventional agrarian practices.[8] Capital gained from trade started to supplant the profits gained from farming. One result of this shift was an increased tolerance for financial speculation and risk. As Craig Muldrew has demonstrated, the escalation in consumption led to a more expansive reliance on networks of debt and credit. He notes that by the end of the sixteenth century many wealthy Englishmen were

> heavily involved in credit networks as increasing expenditure required estate holders to maximize profits from rent and other resources. The great expenses of building, hospitality and other forms of conspicuous expenditure required to define their status competitively meant that they were great borrowers and needed a great deal of credit.[9]

In their desire to maintain their estates, then, landowners in Shakespeare's day began to seek out new kinds of economic flexibility, and they were increasingly lured by the potentially massive returns promised by foreign trade. As a result of these economic changes, risk became more and more central to everyday economic life, and the ability to make a living through investments or trade rather than through manual labour became far more common than it once was.

Global trade and colonialism as well as a general increase in domestic commerce, then, was transforming the nature of work in Shakespeare's England. And with these shifts in economic practices came new ideas about how 'work' should be defined within this rapidly changing commercial environment. The result was an often uneasy relationship between traditional agricultural work and emerging capitalist practices. Indeed, at the same time as the labour associated with commerce, investment, and overseas trade was gaining ascendancy in England, market-based pressures were also transforming more traditional forms of agricultural work. We saw in Chapter 5 how enclosure practices altered traditional relationships with the land, resulting in gains for wealthier landowners at the expense of many tenant farmers. Enclosure threatened longstanding practices of land tillage, characterized by communal, subsistence farming, by shifting emphasis to individual ownership of land in order to maximize profits. The 'honest ploughman' had thus been 'displaced by the thrifty freeholder', as a shift in orientation towards the 'imperatives of a market culture' helped to fundamentally challenge the authority of traditional agricultural labour and customs.[10]

These important changes in how work was understood occurred gradually and unevenly, and they were certainly not embraced by everyone. For instance, some moralists in the period raised significant concerns about the nature of mercantile activity, questioning its legitimacy and whether it counted as 'honest' work. Didn't it seem, for instance, that many merchants reaped profits without performing any labour? Like actors, merchants were one group of people in Shakespeare's England who 'chose to earn a living by practices that not everyone considered to be legitimate'.[11] Some commentators, then, objected to the work of merchants because they were 'troubled by the mysterious nature of commercial profits'.[12] Similar complaints were made about usury—the practice of lending money at interest—on the basis that usurers do no work; they, like merchants, set money out for profit, but rely upon the physical labour of others while they remain idle at home.[13] For both the usurer and the merchant, the focus on profits can hide the processes (and the labour) by which those profits are produced, resulting in a kind of magic or sleight of hand, an idea that we will return to later in this chapter.[14] Merchants were accused by peasants and gentry alike of being overly acquisitive and of engaging in dishonest business dealings without regard to traditional custom or practice.[15] However, earning wealth through trade instead of through more conventional land stewardship gradually became a more acceptable practice in the period. As we saw in Chapter 1, writers from the sixteenth century onward began to identify non-manual forms of labour as work on a regular basis, and the Protestant doctrine of vocations helped solidify the idea that work was a social good that must be undertaken by all. In the case of the merchant specifically, many texts from the period 'sought to invent a new image of the merchant as morally upright and socially useful' in order to counter suspicions about idleness or dishonesty.[16] As we will see, Shakespeare participates in that process in part by yoking the image of the merchant or the commercial investor to images of more traditional, and more accepted, forms of agricultural labour.

Negotiating the Work of Commerce on Shakespeare's Stage

Let's first begin with two brief examples that highlight not only how Shakespeare brings mercantile and commercial activity into the fabric of his drama, but also how he draws attention to the uncertainty and unease that often accompanied these activities in the period. Although there are many references to commercial activity in Shakespeare, his only extended dramatic staging of a merchant who specifically works in overseas trade occurs, perhaps not surprisingly, in *The Merchant of Venice*. The play famously opens with the merchant, Antonio, declaring, 'In sooth, I know not why I am so sad' (1.1.1). Although the precise causes of Antonio's melancholy are never fully articulated, his friend Salerio provides one possible explanation:

> Your mind is tossing on the ocean,
> There where your argosies with portly sail,
> Like signors and rich burghers on the flood—
> Or as it were the pageants of the sea—
> Do overpeer the petty traffickers
> That curtsy to them ... (1.1.8–13)

Antonio is an overseas merchant, whose 'argosies' (large merchant ships), are richly outfitted, especially compared with the 'petty traffickers' they meet upon the seas. Indeed, we learn later from Shylock that Antonio has 'an argosy bound to Tripolis, another to the Indies', with a 'third at Mexico' and a 'fourth for England' (1.3.18–20). These ventures signal that Antonio is a wealthy overseas trader with multiple foreign sources of income, but also multiple sites of financial risk. In the opening scene, Solanio agrees with Salerio that Antonio must be worried about his ships, and he emphasizes the high level of risk involved: 'had I such venture forth | The better part of my affections would | Be with my hopes abroad'. Solanio goes on to say that he would scrutinize weather conditions, maps, and 'every object that might make me fear | Misfortune to my ventures' (1.1.15–21). Risk is clearly a central element of Antonio's line of work, and, given that later in the play we learn that his ships with 'rich lading' have been 'wrecked on the narrow seas' (3.1.3–4), the fear of economic misfortune is hardly misplaced.

Antonio is both a merchant investor and a creditor, as he lends money to Bassanio so that he can woo Portia. As Bassanio frankly tells Antonio, 'I have disabled mine estate', meaning that he has squandered his wealth and finds himself in great debt (1.1.123). Bassanio's position highlights the tension between traditional landholding (the maintenance of the estate) and newer capitalist modes of work, including the risky behaviour and debt they sometimes provoke. He turns to Antonio to borrow money both to offset his debts and to build up the necessary credit needed to become a respectable and successful contender for Portia's hand in marriage, a woman he describes as a 'lady richly left' (1.1.161). Bassanio may be a gentleman by birth, in other words, but he still needs a ready supply of money to maintain his credit and social standing. If Antonio invests in overseas trading in search of a profit, Bassanio also turns a 'profit' by using the money loaned to him by Antonio to win a wealthy heiress in marriage. The play thus positions both Antonio and Bassanio as investors and, indeed, as merchant adventurers. As Mark Netzloff has argued, the play 'is situated within a contemporary debate that attempted to justify England's entrance into a colonial economy by uniting the heroic dimension of colonial expansion, a chivalric discourse appealing to England's gentry, with the interests of commerce and capital'. Through romanticized imagery of the 'golden fleece' (1.1.170), for instance, which Bassanio uses to describe Portia as a marital prize, the play helps promote a new, more sanitized image of foreign trade that connects it with heroic virtue rather than vice or debauchery.[17]

We see a similar rhetorical move at play in *Measure for Measure*, where the emphasis is not on foreign trade, but on commercial work in an urban context. The play is set in Vienna, but scholars have noted the connections between *Measure for Measure*'s world of urban commerce and that of Jacobean London, a world frequently represented in the city comedies of playwrights such as Thomas Middleton, Thomas Dekker, and Ben Jonson.[18] The commercial milieu of *Measure for Measure* is established early in the play through the conversation between Lucio and Mistress Overdone, who finds herself 'custom-shrunk' due to a lack of customers at her brothel, the result of the recent proclamations against sexual vice made by the Duke (1.2.82). Commercial work is not the only kind of labour to be found in this play, however. Amidst *Measure for Measure*'s world of urban trade, Shakespeare also provides a few striking images of agricultural labour to describe romantic love and procreation. As we saw in the previous chapter, Shakespeare in his green world plays often uses images of agrarian work to describe romantic or sexual maturity. In *Measure for Measure*, we find a similar pattern, but in a decidedly urban rather than green world setting. For instance, when explaining to Isabella that her brother Claudio has got his fiancée Juliet with child, he says:

> Your brother and his lover have embraced.
> As those that feed grow full, as blossoming time
> That from the seedness the bare fallow brings
> To teeming foison, even so her plenteous womb
> Expresseth his full tilth and husbandry. (1.4.39–43)

Lucio describes Claudio and Juliet's pregnancy in terms of the process of ripening and harvesting necessary to agricultural production. 'Seedness' refers to sowing, which transforms the barrow 'fallow' (ploughland) into 'foison', or abundance, through 'tilth', or the cultivation of the land through manual labour. Shakespeare here uses an agricultural metaphor to depict heterosexual procreation, much as he did in *Twelfth Night* and *The Tempest*, as we saw in Chapter 5.

Later in the play, when the Duke is explaining to Mariana and Isabella his plan for the bed trick, in which Mariana will substitute for Isabella in bed with Angelo in order to preserve Isabella's honour and enable Mariana and Angelo to be reunited in marriage, he uses a similar agrarian image. He tells the women: 'Our corn's to reap, for yet our tilth's to sow' (4.1.74). Once again, the labour of the harvest provides imaginative context for the complex endgame envisioned and managed by the Duke, through which he seeks to restore order via heterosexual marriage. Yoking agricultural labour to the romantic trajectory of comedy, these agrarian images in *Measure for Measure* temporarily reset the mood of this highly urban and commercial play, returning us momentarily to the world of pastoral romance and retreat examined in Chapter 5. Like the reference to Portia as the 'golden fleece' in *The Merchant of Venice*, which de-emphasizes the more commercial elements of the romantic plotline in favour of a story of heroic adventure, this language of harvest invokes a nostalgic, romanticized image of rural labour as a sharp contrast to *Measure for Measure*'s seedy urban setting. Instead of emphasizing credit relations, commercial trade, and the details of the urban economy that constitute Vienna in the play, Shakespeare connects the comedy's romantic trajectories with pastoral agriculture, thereby distancing these relationships from the taint of commerce. These examples from *The Merchant of Venice* and *Measure for Measure* indicate how Shakespeare could deploy figurative language in his plays to offset the perceived stigma of commercial exchange or mercantile labour. In the remainder of this chapter, we will explore this process in greater detail as we consider how images of agricultural labour help justify or reframe the work of commercial enterprise, both domestic and foreign.

Agriculture, Romance, and Commercial Labour

Two of Shakespeare's late romances, *The Winter's Tale* and *The Tempest*, feature striking scenes and images of rural labour. As we saw in the previous chapter, both of these plays turn to agrarian imagery to highlight comedic development and the pathways of romantic love. But both plays also use agricultural imagery for an additional purpose: to rhetorically soften the commercial exchanges that they stage. In Act 4 of *The Winter's Tale*, for instance, the pastoral setting in Bohemia, centred around a sheep-shearing festival, draws the audience into an idyllic, rural setting. But it also highlights the tension between more traditional forms of rural agriculture and newer, commercial forms of labour. Act 4, scene 3 opens with the rogue Autolycus, a self-described tinker (a mender of metal pots and household goods, like Sly in *The Taming of the Shrew*), singing a ditty that invokes innocent rural pleasures and seasonality:

> When daffodils begin to peer,
> With heigh, the doxy over the dale,
> Why then comes in the sweet o' the year,
> For the red blood reigns in the winter's pale. (4.3.1–4)

The invocation of the seasons sets the stage for the summer sheep-shearing festival to come in the following scene, promising a pastoral retreat grounded in the cyclical pattern of agricultural work. However, Autolycus quickly reveals that his own motives for attending the festival are less than innocent. Autolycus is a lower-order labourer as well as a buyer and seller of cheap goods, but he is also a con artist and petty thief. During an exchange with the Clown, the Old Shepard's son, Autolycus steals his money and decides to use the upcoming festival as an occasion to steal more, bragging that he will make the 'shearers prove sheep' (4.3.121). Autolycus' status as an itinerant rogue who has served Prince Florizel in the past but is currently 'out of service' (4.3.14) links him to the vagrancy and idleness that was so decried by Elizabethan and Jacobean authorities, as we saw in Chapter 1. If Autolycus represents a commercial intrusion into the pastoral retreat of rural Bohemia, the play suggests that his actions could pose a potential threat to social order.

However, it's too simple to view Autolycus as merely an intrusion or an anomaly. The pastoral activities of Act 4 clearly demonstrate that rural labour is fully entwined with commerce, not separate from it. When Autolycus first meets the Clown, for instance, we learn that the sheep-shearing festival itself relies directly on trade and commodity exchange. The Clown has been sent by his father to buy a host of supplies for the feast, including 'three pound of sugar, five pound of currants', as well as rice, saffron, dates, ginger, and other spices (4.3.36–17). And during the festival scene that follows, we see on stage far more buying and selling of petty goods than other forms of rural labour.

Autolycus enters the festival as an itinerant salesman of sorts, offering up ballads as well as fabric, clothing, and other personal goods for purchase. His entrance song at the feast highlights the commercial labour he brings to this gathering:

> Lawn as white as driven snow,
> Cypress black as e'er was crow,
> Gloves as sweet as damask roses,
> Masks for faces, and for noses;
> Bugle-bracelet, necklace amber,
> Perfume for a lady's chamber;
> Golden coifs, and stomachers
> For my lads to give their dears;
> Pins and poking-sticks of steel,
> What maids lack from head to heel
> Come buy of me, come, come buy, come buy,
> Buy, lads, or else your lasses cry. Come buy! (4.4.219–30)

Autolycus directly connects the buying and selling of goods—here a mix of cheaper wares and more luxurious items, including foreign imports such as amber—with romantic pursuit, urging 'lads' to buy goods in order to win their 'lasses'. Furthermore, the rural participants at the festival eagerly embrace Autolycus' commercial spirit. Although the main protagonists Florizel and Perdita pointedly reject the commercial trade of 'such trifles' (4.4.355), Mopsa, Dorcus, and the Clown readily engage in the back-and-forth process of bartering and purchasing. And yet, if the scene puts trade and commercial labour centre stage, the agricultural setting is still a crucial feature of Shakespeare's dramaturgy. The context of agrarian labour and seasonal festivity that clearly frames this lengthy scene effectively enables Shakespeare to explore a commercial 'politics of self interest' in a way that lessens its negative force.[19] The highly romanticized images of shepherds and rural labour that form the backdrop to this festival help to soften the commercial elements of the scene. Similarly, the rollicking rhythms of Autolycus' merry festival songs, linked to cultural practices associated with the rural economy, offset the world of domestic and foreign trade of which he sings. The play may not overtly applaud Autolycus' rogue behaviour, but neither does it exclude him from its conclusion: Autolycus ultimately helps (albeit somewhat reluctantly) to bring the romantic plot and the lost-daughter plot to a successful resolution. Shakespeare thus creates a fictional world in which the tensions between traditional rural work and newer commercial practices can coexist, with the former helping to justify the latter. By yoking sheep-shearing and mercantile activities together, Shakespeare in *The Winter's Tale* both showcases and lends credibility to some of the new labour practices of a growing consumer economy.

In *The Tempest*, the masque of Ceres that Prospero orchestrates in Act 4 similarly highlights agricultural labour and contrasts it with the labour of colonialism and foreign venture that is the primary context for the play's island setting. In the previous chapter, we saw how the masque celebrates marital fecundity through images of agricultural bounty and harvest, imposing a sense of order and respite on the otherwise chaotic activities of the island's green world setting. But the agricultural labour highlighted in the masque also provides a comforting image of traditional, rural economic practices that helps to offset potential concerns about Prospero's control of the island. Joining Juno in song, Ceres proclaims:

> Earth's increase, and foison plenty,
> Barns and garners never empty,
> Vines with clust'ring bunches growing,
> Plants with goodly burden bowing;
> Spring come to you at the farthest,
> In the very end of harvest.
> Scarcity and want shall shun you,
> Ceres' blessing so is on you. (4.1.110–17)

In the middle of a seemingly barren island landscape, Prospero magically invokes a 'distinctly English countryside, marked by nibbling sheep, agrarian husbandry, and enclosed fields'.[20] The images of mixed farming (i.e. the production of arable crops in addition to the raising of livestock) in the masque's exchange between Iris and Ceres laud distinctly English forms of agricultural labour. Ceres in particular, as Charlotte Scott has observed, 'occupied a vivid role in the English cultural imagination' because of how she 'could represent, in heavenly form, agrarian industry as a shared human and non-human goal'.[21] And while the allusions to enclosure might remind audiences of the economic realities of contemporary English agricultural practices and disputes about landownership and use rights (as we saw in Chapter 5), those concerns are deflected by the tone of celebration and festivity that characterizes the scene. Interestingly, Ceres' vision of agrarian plenty also defies the typical calendrical cycle, an alteration that heightens the focus on agricultural work in her blessing, even while that work is heavily romanticized. In wishing that spring will come to the young couple at the 'very end of harvest', Ceres skips over the winter part of the year, opting instead for a 'perpetual alternation of spring and summer'.[22] By modifying the traditional seasonal calendar, Ceres' vision centres attention on the two seasons in which the most labour-intensive agricultural work—the work of sowing, weeding, shearing, and harvesting—was performed. The altered temporality of Ceres' vision thus doubles down on the images of agricultural labour that permeate Prospero's masque. But in doing so, the song highlights the products of labour ('foison plenty' and 'barns and garners never empty') instead of the human actions that produced them. In Prospero's carefully arranged masque, agrarian work is both celebrated and sentimentalized.

Ferdinand immediately responds to Ceres' romanticized tribute to English agrarianism by calling it a 'most majestic vision' (118). A few lines later, 'certain Reapers, properly habited' appear onstage during Prospero's spectacle for Ferdinand and Miranda. Once again, the labour of harvesting crops is joined to festivity and celebration, as the reapers 'join with the Nymphs in a graceful dance' (4.1.138 s.d.). Agrarian labour is thus romanticized in order to emphasize harmony, marital joy, and community rather than laborious effort or the practical struggles of everyday workers. As Scott has argued, through the masque, 'cultivation appears magical, transformative, and capable of generating produce and plenty where none exists'.[23] She goes on to note that Prospero's references to the cultivation of the English rural landscape help to construct a positive vision of social order based on a shared set of social and economic values.[24]

The images of agrarian labour in the masque help establish order at a crucial moment in the play, but they also help to offset and justify the more commercial and colonial forms of labour that make Prospero's rule possible. Although he is unable to cultivate the island on his own, in the masque Prospero 'reproduces the work of the husbandman in illusion'.[25] Prospero builds strategically on images of rural labour to create and sustain his magical spectacle, a performance that he describes as a 'vanity of mine art' (4.1.41), while simultaneously relying on the labour of his 'industrious servant, Ariel' (4.1.33) to create the illusion. As the reference to Ariel suggests, this is not simply a magic act, but a display of Prospero's power that is dependent upon the processes of colonial trade and foreign ventures that underwrite his settlement of the island. As we saw in our discussion of service and slavery in Chapter 3, Prospero may not come to the island explicitly as a colonizer, but his actions 'fit the colonial paradigm' in terms of his enforced bondage of Ariel and Caliban and his appropriation of the island's natural resources.[26] The play clearly separates Prospero as the ruler of the island and the manager of its land from those who actively work the land for him, namely Ariel and, especially, Caliban. As Patricia Akhimie has argued, it is Caliban's daily work of agrarian husbandry that 'allows audiences to believe that an old man and young girl might survive on a barren island for 12 years' time'.[27] In the masque, however, the romanticized images of agrarian labour, encapsulated in the figures of Ceres and the dancing reapers, help buttress Prospero's power, giving the illusion that his control over the island is grounded not in the enforcement of colonial labour practices or in the risky ventures of overseas trade and exploration, but rather in the traditional, safe economic practices of agrarian husbandry. Furthermore, the magical, even whimsical performance of agricultural labour in the masque further elides the actual labour (such as Caliban's carrying of logs for firewood) that occurs on the island, offering instead only a romantic, mystified version of traditional rural labour practices.[28]

In *The Tempest*, then, Shakespeare uses romanticized images of agrarian labour and specific references to English agricultural traditions to render more palatable the work of mercantile trade, foreign travel, and colonial enterprise that forms a crucial backdrop for the play. Much like the references to the golden fleece in *The Merchant of Venice*, the agrarian images of Ceres' masque help to ground colonialism and foreign trade in more reassuring terms, constituting a kind of poetic management of the tensions and potential disruptions associated with mercantile activity in Shakespeare's England. Writing about the increasingly arduous labour of foreign travel in the period, Daniel

Vitkus has suggested that the power and influence of the 'new commercial classes' helped to stimulate forms of cultural and literary discourses that 'could provide ideological support for their enterprises'. In plays from the period, he argues, the physical labour of travel gets abstracted and instead presented on stage as an adventure.[29] We see a similar dramatic process at work in *The Tempest*, where the labour of travelling to, colonializing, and maintaining the island is elided and replaced not in this case with the motif of adventure, but instead with the idealized, even magical vision of traditional agrarian husbandry.

Chestnuts and Harvest-Home

Understanding how Shakespeare uses images of agricultural labour to defray potential concerns about newer forms of commercial labour, including trade, foreign investment, and the mercantile work associated with English colonialism, as we saw in *The Winter's Tale* and *The Tempest*, can also help us make sense of some of Shakespeare's more transient allusions, references that may at first appear insignificant, but that can nevertheless offer rich insights into Shakespeare's dramaturgy. As we saw in Shakespeare's use of the phrase 'clubs, clubs' in Chapter 4, Shakespeare can deploy quick and seemingly offhand references to labour and put them to significant effect, establishing character, tone, and the dramatic import of a scene. We can see a similar process at work in Shakespeare's use of individual words that borrow from the world of agricultural labour. These references may be brief, but they pack a big punch: Shakespeare can use them to conjure up a range of agrarian contexts and instantly convey them to audiences in order to heighten the effect of a scene, speech, or character exchange. One such example occurs in *Macbeth*, a play that seems far removed from the world of rural agriculture. And yet, we can see how even a single-word reference to an individual food product can showcase in miniature the tension between traditional forms of agrarian work and newer practices of foreign trade and mercantile labour.

In Act 1 of *Macbeth*, the three witches converse obliquely about a sailor's wife and their plans to pursue her husband abroad. The first witch recounts:

A sailor's wife had chestnuts in her lap,
And munched, and munched, and munched. 'Give me,' quoth I.
'Aroint thee, witch,' the rump-fed runnion cries.
Her husband's to Aleppo gone, Master o' th' Tiger.
  But in a sieve I'll thither sail,
  And like a rat without a tail
  I'll do, I'll do, and I'll do. (1.3.3–9)

It's easy to read the witch's rhythmic verses as a form of poetic enchantment without giving much attention to the specific details included within the lines. However, I'd encourage us to pause for a moment at the mention of the chestnuts to think further about how Shakespeare might be using this reference at this particular dramatic moment. Why chestnuts? What might the mention of chestnuts have evoked for members of Shakespeare's audience? Chestnuts were a fascinating food product in the early modern period precisely because they were a kind of hybrid: they could simultaneously bring to mind images of traditional subsistence agriculture as well as more sophisticated practices of global trade. On the one hand, what we now refer to as the sweet chestnut (*castanea sativa*) was a significant food source for many rural peasants throughout the early modern period, especially in Balkan and Mediterranean countries. Chestnuts ground into flour could be used to make bread when other grains were scarce.[30] Harvesting and collecting chestnuts was manual and communal work, and, because chestnuts were quite perishable, they were either eaten shortly after collection (which usually entailed a time-intensive peeling procedure before they were boiled), or they were dried (typically by being smoked), which made peeling much easier and allowed them to be preserved for many months, even years.[31] The witches' mention of chestnuts could thus have called to mind images of communal, subsistence agricultural work.

On the other hand, the chestnut could also have evoked images of foreign trade and luxury imports. Part of the discrepancy here lies in the different varieties of chestnuts that would have been available in Shakespeare's England. For instance, ordinary sweet chestnuts were distinguished at times from the larger *marrons*, most of which would have been imported from France or Spain in Shakespeare's day. *Marrons* were considered expensive delicacies enjoyed by the wealthy and historically 'commanded a price three or four times greater than their common…counterparts'.[32] Furthermore, although chestnuts were cultivated in England by Shakespeare's time, many would still likely have been imported from countries such as Italy, where the climate was more conducive to their growth.[33] The reference to the sailor who travels to Aleppo in the witch's account further activates images of global trade and the work of maritime commerce. The witch's reference to chestnuts thus may have evoked images of exotic foodstuffs and foreign trade at the same time as it reminded audiences of the labour of subsistence farming.

The chestnut as a hybrid food product—at once both domestic and foreign—draws attention to the complex ways in which domestic labour and food production were increasingly shaped by global developments in the period. The chestnut perfectly encapsulates the widening gap in Shakespeare's England between subsistence agriculture and production, on the one hand, and market-based trade and consumption, on the other, as well as the ongoing tensions between the two. The chestnut is simultaneously a basic food product and an object that suggests how the English labour economy has been transformed through its involvement in global trade. Furthermore, like the masque in *The Tempest*, the witch's story downplays the intense, risky labours (including the labour of travel itself) associated with colonialism and the maritime economy. Instead, we get an account of the sailor's wife eating (and refusing to share) her chestnuts, and a fanciful description of the witch's own magical transport to Aleppo ('in a sieve I'll thither sail'). In this brief moment, we catch a glimpse of the process by which early modern foodstuffs are being gradually dissociated from the labour that produces them. This process is similar to what we saw in *The Tempest*, where Prospero separates his command of the island from the colonial labour that enables it. We might think of the reference to the chestnut in *Macbeth*, then, as a kind of poetic time capsule. Through this single image, Shakespeare brilliantly captures the tensions between traditional agrarian labour and newer forms of commercial work that were coming to a head in early modern England. And he does this without showcasing either type of labour directly on the stage.

Let's now turn to one final example that can help bring together some of the threads explored throughout this chapter. In Shakespeare's

The Merry Wives of Windsor, a brief but pointed allusion to harvesting brings agrarian labour suddenly and unexpectedly into the play, a romantic comedy set not in an idealized pastoral landscape (like the Forest of Arden in *As You Like It*), but in the English town of Windsor. By analysing Shakespeare's use of the phrase 'harvest-home', we can trace how agrarian labour shapes the comedic fabric of this play, written and performed, as this chapter has demonstrated, when England was gradually moving from an exclusively agrarian to a mixed economy increasingly dependent on trade, consumer goods, and financial risk. Like the chestnut in *Macbeth*, the reference to 'harvest-home' in *Merry Wives* draws attention to contemporary agricultural practices, but in this case the image is used to describe the nefarious actions of its most famous character: Falstaff.

In Act 2, scene 2 of *Merry Wives*, Master Ford, disguised as Master Brooke, pays Falstaff to woo his wife on his behalf, in an effort to test her marital fidelity. Explaining his plan to dupe Ford in order to get to his 'masses of money', Falstaff tells the supposed Master Brooke: 'I will use her as the key of the cuckoldry rogue's coffer, and there's my harvest-home' (2.2.262–5). Harvest-home was the name of a rural, agricultural festival, usually held in England at the end of August. Most of the labour in the fields was carried out during the second half of the calendar year, running from 25 June to 24 December. That same period was punctuated by a series of secular festivals in which villagers and rural labourers celebrated the completion of work. The sheep-shearing festival in early summer (as featured in *The Winter's Tale*) was followed by the rush-bearing festival in July, by harvest-home in August, and finally by hop-picking in autumn.[34] All of these festivals were, of course, celebratory events that emphasized leisure and play, but they were also closely connected to the specific labours that preceded them. Of these four kinds of agricultural work, harvesting was by far the longest in overall duration, with only the final day of the harvest being devoted to celebration. As François Laroque describes the event in *Shakespeare's Festive World*: 'The festival began with the decoration of the very last wheat-sheaf and the wagon that was to carry it to the barn where it would be stored. The cheery procession that accompanied the last waggon of wheat signalled the end of the harvesting and storage of the crop, the "harvest-home" as it was known, and opened the public rejoicings.' The revelry associated with harvest-home marked 'the combined efforts of the rural population in bringing in and storing the harvest'.[35]

There is only one other mention of 'harvest-home' in Shakespeare, and it occurs in *1 Henry IV*. When Hotspur is complaining to the King about the behaviour of the courtier who comes to the battlefield to demand his prisoners, Hotspur describes him derogatorily as a lord who was 'neat and trimly dressed, | Fresh as a bridegroom, and his chin, new-reaped, | Showed like a stubble-land at harvest-home' (1.3.32–4). Both Shakespearian uses of 'harvest-home' are metaphoric, and both are incongruous within their narrative setting (the description of a battlefield in *1 Henry IV* or of a wooing plot in *Merry Wives*). So, what work might this metaphor be doing? On its surface, Hotspur's reference simply suggests that the lord is a freshly shaved youth not suited for fighting. Hotspur thus verbally disparages the courtier by implying that he is poorly prepared for war and not cut out for martial valour: he is a shallow sycophant who is out of place on the battlefield. However, Hotspur also denigrates the courtier by describing his appearance in terms of rural labour that is already completed ('new-reaped') rather than ongoing. He is not an active worker, in other words, but merely someone who reaps the benefits of labour that has already been completed. Furthermore, the celebration of harvest-home was frequently described in the period as a sexually and socially promiscuous occasion. Summarizing reports from travellers visiting England, Laroque notes: 'Men and women mingled together, as did masters and servants, just as they had worked alongside one another in the fields.'[36] The carnivalesque nature of harvest-home further supports Hotspur's denigration of the courtier as one who resorts to 'holiday and lady terms' (1.3.45) not properly suited to the gravitas of battle. If we return to *Merry Wives*, this association with carnival and festival certainly seems appropriate for Falstaff as well, given his larger-than-life comedic personality and his overt flouting of proprietary norms. His attempts to woo Mistresses Page and Ford in *Merry Wives* might very well be viewed as carnivalesque actions.[37]

But Falstaff's reference to 'harvest-home' is more than just an offhand moment of festive light-heartedness. For one thing, this allusion encapsulates in miniature one of the primary comic arcs of the play: it characterizes the pursuit of Mistress Ford as the labour that will result in a celebratory festival, that is (in this case) sexual consummation.

And while such sexual conquest may indeed be Falstaff's main goal, that carnivalesque impulse is only possible within a dramatic framework in which labour is the necessary prerequisite for communal leisure. Falstaff's reference to 'harvest-home', in other words, invokes a fundamental opposition between work and leisure, but it also reminds us that one (work) is required before the other (leisure) can occur. Falstaff's boast to Ford (disguised as Brooke) marks a crucial moment in the main plot of *Merry Wives*, one that sets a plan in motion and foreshadows a possible comedic endpoint in the successful wooing of Mistress Ford. What's notable here is that the temporal rhythms of agricultural labour provide the necessary frame for Falstaff's plotting, and, in turn, an important context for understanding the play's comedic trajectory. The metaphor of wooing as harvesting suggests that an acceptance of temporal patterns based in the rhythms of an agrarian calendar is necessary to comic conclusion, a formula that we saw in plays such as *As You Like It* and *Love's Labour's Lost*, as discussed in Chapter 5.

But Falstaff's specific usage, and what we know of his character throughout the play, also hint at a more mercenary impulse: a deployment of imagery from rural labour to justify an act of deception in the interest of economic gain. He pursues Mistress Ford, after all, to get 'the key of the cuckoldry rogue's coffer'. Falstaff here uses agricultural work to underwrite a very different kind of activity, and one that is specifically open to moral scrutiny: a confidence scheme (or, in Falstaff's case, an attempted one). As we've seen, the growth of English consumerism and the marked increase in mercantile activity during this period led to the assumption of greater economic risk than was true in previous generations. And just as Shakespeare in plays such as *The Tempest* and *The Winter's Tale* uses images of agrarian labour to help soften or justify newer forms of mercantile work, we can see a similar pattern compressed within Falstaff's seemingly innocuous reference to 'harvest-home'. Falstaff, after all, is a con artist in much the same way as Autolycus is in *The Winter's Tale*. In that play, we saw that Shakespeare uses images of rural labour to help temper the negative force of Autolycus' mercenary activities: Autolycus' rhyming pastoral songs, for instance, draw attention away from his covetous motives. In *Merry Wives*, Falstaff similarly relies upon the ethical promise of rural husbandry encoded in the concept of 'harvest-home' to justify his economic gamesmanship. Falstaff strategically uses the image of the harvest, in other words, to make himself appear more credible in his conversation with Ford/Brooke. If Falstaff is a swindler, one who seeks to take advantage of market forces and commercial risk for his own gain, then his allusion to the harvest substitutes a more comforting, traditional image of manual labour in order to positively reframe the ethical value of his actions.

The play overall, however, is ambivalent about Falstaff's efforts to reframe the labour of harvest for ends that are potentially suspect. The ultimate shaming of Falstaff at Herne's Oak subordinates him socially, physically, and economically by casting him as the figure of Herne the Hunter, the spirit of a former gamekeeper of Windsor Forest linked to hunting mythology, but whom Mistress Page also describes as harming livestock and disrupting rural labour. She says that superstitious people believe that Herne 'blasts the trees, and takes the cattle, | And makes milch-kine [i.e. dairy cattle] yield blood' (4.4.31–2). In addition to the overt connection to cuckoldry that Herne's wearing of horns suggests, the role is an especially appropriate 'harvest-home' for Falstaff: a festive conclusion, just not on his terms. In its carnivalesque conclusion, the play depicts Falstaff not as the lusty harvester he himself envisioned earlier in the play, but rather as someone who disrupts rural husbandry in much the same way he has upset domestic harmony. In this sense, Falstaff's punishment restores more traditional social order. Indeed, during the final scene, Mistress Quickly, disguised as the Fairy Queen, commands her fairies to bless Windsor Castle, using language that emphasizes fertility ('fertile-fresh' [5.5.67]) and communal festivity as they dance together around the oak tree. Denying Falstaff's impulse to use the imagery of the harvest to justify his confidence scheme against the wives, the play instead returns us to an idea of community that is secured by a nostalgic version of rural labour. Once again, the language of agrarian labour enables Shakespeare to impose dramatic order on leisure, idleness, and wildness.

If we consider only staged action, there would be very little to say about agricultural work in *Merry Wives.* However, in the brief yet resonant mention of 'harvest-home', we find that the language of agrarian labour influences the plotting and themes of this comedy in surprising ways. Falstaff uses the language of rural labour in *Merry Wives* to create a nostalgic through-line that helps to justify his economic scheming, even though the play as a whole rejects his duplicitous financial motives. In the fictional world of Windsor, Falstaff performs a dramatic sleight-of-hand, drawing our attention to traditional agrarian labour practices as a way of temporarily offsetting and productively reframing the riskier and even at times unsavoury work that often went hand in hand with England's developing commercial economy. Like the phrase 'clubs, clubs' that we discussed in Chapter 4 and the single mention of chestnuts in *Macbeth*, Falstaff's reference to 'harvest-home' demonstrates the value of attending to Shakespeare's language of labour, even when labour is not the primary focus of a given scene. Through these examples, we can see just how extensively work permeates Shakespeare's dramatic language, animating his plots, themes, characters, and dialogue. By exploring these moments, we can not only develop new interpretations of the plays, but also cultivate a deeper understanding of how Shakespeare's dramatic craft was profoundly shaped by his 'working words'.

Shakespeare and Work. Michelle M. Dowd, Oxford University Press. © Michelle M. Dowd 2026.
DOI: 10.1093/9780191998096.003.0007

Epilogue: Shakespeare's Working Words

In his autobiography, J. R. Clynes (1869–1949), a working-class son of a farmworker in Oldham, England, who later became a member of Parliament, recalls an incident in which Shakespeare helped him successfully negotiate a labour strike. An avid reader of Shakespeare in his spare time, Clynes, in his role as a trade union official, was asked to negotiate a strike with a particularly uncooperative employer. As he describes the encounter: 'With considerable persistence I succeeded in obtaining an interview with him. I quoted a line from *Much Ado About Nothing*, and he stared in astonishment. Then we plunged into a discussion about Shakespeare's comedies, which lasted us till luncheon was announced.' After lunch, Clynes continues to make good on his knowledge of Shakespeare to impress the employer: 'So, when the coffee cups had been removed, I declaimed the whole of one longish scene from *Julius Caesar* to him.' At the end of the discussion, Clynes brought the topic back to the labour strike. The employer swiftly concedes the workers' demands, enabling Clynes to tell his fellow workers 'the good news that the concessions for which they had decided to fight were granted'.[1] Clynes's knowledge of Shakespeare thus scores a win for workers' rights, a remarkable turn of events that may seem far-fetched to us today. But in the late-nineteenth-century world that Clynes describes, Shakespeare was a shared reference point for many working-class readers, including those involved in the various labour and reform movements of the period, such as Chartism. For many workers such as Clynes, Shakespeare was not viewed as a highbrow artist to be read exclusively in elite circles, but as a writer who was very much an ally of the working classes.[2]

What might account for this embrace of Shakespeare by working-class readers in the nineteenth century? Certainly, readers in earlier periods did not always assume an affinity between Shakespeare and work. As we saw in Chapter 2, seventeenth- and eighteenth-century commentators often tended to value Shakespeare precisely because he (in their opinion) did *not work*, at least as a writer. Instead, his creative genius was understood as a pure product of his imagination, an effortless endeavour. As John Dryden noted in 1668, for Shakespeare, 'All the Images of Nature were still present to him, and he drew them not laboriously, but luckily.'[3] Certainly not all early readers or theatregoers agreed with this assessment. As discussed in Chapter 4, apprentices and unemployed workers regularly went to see Shakespeare's plays in the late sixteenth and early seventeenth centuries, and Ben Jonson's commendatory poem in the 1623 First Folio, considered in Chapter 2, emphasizes Shakespeare as a craftsman, an idea that matches what we now know about Shakespeare's practices as a working artist. And yet, for much of the Restoration and eighteenth century, Shakespeare was more commonly viewed as a poet of nature, rather than one who was interested in the everyday world of work. Such perceptions went hand in hand with changes to theatrical practices during these periods, which included a shift to more private theatres, an emphasis on neoclassical principles of decorum, and a focus on aristocratic literary and cultural perspectives.[4]

All of this changed by the nineteenth century. During this period, Shakespeare's mass appeal was arguably at the highest it has ever been.[5] Why? One significant reason was that changes in education as well as in publishing and theatrical practices had a significant impact on who could access Shakespeare. In England, increased government funding for schools meant that even the poorest children could obtain some form of education. A general rise in literacy and the increased presence of secular reading materials, including quotations from Shakespeare, in schools also spurred an interest in extracurricular reading.[6] At the same time, the increasing availability of cheap books and journals helped 'to nurture the reading habit among those who received an elementary education within the gradually expanding school network'.[7] Among these cheap publications were editions of Shakespeare, which dropped significantly in price during this period so that by the second half of the nineteenth century, 'Shakespeare had become readily affordable even to those on the most modest of incomes'.[8] In the theatre too, Shakespeare was broadly considered to be popular entertainment in nineteenth-century England and

America. Theatregoers represented nearly all ranks of society, and performances often involved active audience participation.[9]

These socio-economic developments during the nineteenth century led directly to the more political uses of Shakespeare by members of the working classes. In his overview of the 'political appropriation of Shakespeare outside the theatre', beginning in the eighteenth century and extending into the nineteenth, Jonathan Bate notes:

> The increasing popularity of the plays on stage and the multiplication of printed editions meant that Shakespeare had become sufficiently well known, especially in educated and hence politically conscious circles in London, for allusions to his words to be recognizable and to exercise the kind of authorizing function previously reserved for classical tags. Shakespearean allusion thus became an available resource in political discourse.[10]

We see this dynamic at work in the Clynes example with which I started, but there are many other fascinating examples from the period of working-class affinity for Shakespeare's words. In 1848, Ernest Jones, an imprisoned leader of the working-class Chartist movement for political reform, requested a copy of Shakespeare's tragedies to read for both comfort and inspiration while he was in solitary confinement. His request was denied. In the 1870s and 1880s, the leader of the Agricultural Laborers' Union, Joseph Arch, a radical reformer from Warwickshire who was politically appealing to many agricultural workers in the region, quoted Shakespeare frequently in his speeches. For Arch, Shakespeare's life offered an example for agricultural labourers who were connected to the soil and 'striving for self-improvement'.[11]

Perhaps the best-known example of working-class alignment with Shakespeare occurred in America: the infamous Astor Place riots of 1849. On 7 May of that year, two very different Shakespearian actors performed in separate, competing performances of *Macbeth* in New York City. Edwin Forrest, an American actor known for his 'vigorous acting style' and his championing of 'self-improvement and social mobility', which endeared him to populist American audiences, performed at the Broadway Theatre. William Charles Macready, an English actor with a 'cerebral' acting style and an 'aristocratic demeanor', performed at the Astor Place Opera House. During his performance, Macready was so aggressively heckled by the audience—not only by boos, but also by 'an avalanche of eggs, apples, potatoes, lemons, and, ultimately, chairs hurled from the gallery', that he was forced to leave the stage and halt the performance. Three days later, Macready again performed *Macbeth* at the Astor Place Opera House to a full house. During the performance, an angry crowd that had formed outside attempted to storm the theatre, but was stopped by militia, who fired point-blank into the crowd. In the end, twenty-one people were killed.[12] Members of the working classes played a notable role in the protests, stirred up by their antipathy towards Macready and what they saw as his aristocratic appropriation of Shakespeare. If the eighty-six men arrested following the riots were representative of the larger crowd, then it had been composed primarily of working men, including butchers, carpenters, clerks, plumbers, and other labourers. As one speaker at a rally held the day after the incident claimed, the 'murder' of the men during the riot was done 'to revenge the aristocrats of this city against the working classes'.[13] The Astor Place riots, along with the other examples I've given here, demonstrate just how strong working-class affinities for Shakespeare could be. Not only were Shakespeare's works deployed strategically for radical political ends in the period, but in some circles 'Shakespeare was granted the status of a card-carrying member of the working class.'[14]

Once again, all of this would change as the nineteenth century gave way to the twentieth and the twenty-first. As always, these changes were gradual and complex, but by the first few decades of the twentieth century, the high level of working-class investment in Shakespeare that was seen in the nineteenth century began to diminish. Changes in educational practices and in the fields of publishing and theatrical performance help account for many of these shifts. For instance, as the twentieth century progressed, Shakespeare increasingly became the purview of the formal educational curriculum, at both the secondary and post-secondary levels. Over time, this change helped establish 'a connection between the playwright and a gradually emerging conception of an elite culture that distinguished itself from its populist counterpart'.[15] Rather than being an author read voraciously and informally, as was the case for many working-class readers in the nineteenth century, Shakespeare became the 'subject of disciplinary knowledge, requirements, and examinations'.[16] Shakespeare studies, including the practices of editing and criticism, became increasingly professionalized during the twentieth century, creating a hierarchy in which Shakespeare was more frequently aligned with elite than with popular or working-class culture.

Similar changes occurred in the theatre. In the twentieth century, theatregoing became much less of an activity that 'embodied all classes within a shared public space', and Shakespearian theatre in particular was established as serious and elite, in opposition to the more popular forms of theatre (such as vaudeville and slapstick) with which it had often been aligned in the nineteenth century.[17] Shakespearian theatre thus gradually became a feature of twentieth-century high culture, associated with intelligence and discernment rather than popular entertainment as such. In addition, new developments in media and other forms of entertainment helped to spur this bifurcation of culture. By the early decades of the twentieth century, film had already begun to displace theatre as a popular form of entertainment. Even as early as 1915, as Lawrence W. Levine recounts, 'a worker could take his wife and three children to the movies for the price of one gallery seat at the regular theatre'.[18] Of course, these trends in new media only escalated as the century progressed, so that by our own twenty-first century, mass media in multiple forms (including not only television and film, but also podcasts, video games, and social media, to name just a few) have displaced traditional theatre as a form of popular entertainment.

So, what does all of this have to do with Shakespeare and work? I'd like to suggest that a recognition of Shakespeare's transformation from an artist beloved by working-class readers and audiences in the nineteenth century to one perceived as a bastion of 'high' culture can help us to better understand our own perceptions of Shakespeare and his relationship to work from our positions as students, readers, and audiences in the twenty-first century. As a basic point, we can see that Shakespeare's perceived relationship to work has not been static, but has changed over time with shifts in historical and social circumstances, including changes to both popular and elite cultural forms. At the same time, we should be careful of overstating this divide between 'high' and 'low' culture, especially given that our own contemporary moment is marked by a degree of flexibility and cultural eclecticism that is distinctive. Shakespeare pervades many aspects of our world, ranging from the quotidian (memes, soundbites) to the broadly popular (film adaptations, graphic novels) to the more elite (traditional theatre, formal curricula). Indeed, one of the factors that has contributed to Shakespeare's status as a part of 'elite' culture—his ubiquitous presence in the education system—has also contributed to his pervasiveness throughout culture more broadly. As Denise Albanese has noted, Shakespeare is part of a public culture 'precisely because the mass-educational project of the twentieth century made him so'.[19] And so, it is perhaps fair to say that Shakespeare today is at once more accessible and popular than he was in previous centuries and yet also more elite, in that he is no longer associated with popular labour movements as he was in the nineteenth century, but more frequently with other forms of 'high' culture. But despite the fact that the hierarchical lines between 'high' and 'low' culture in our current moment are far less sharply drawn than they were in the nineteenth and twentieth centuries, it is still worth considering whether there remains, at least for some readers and students, a vestige of truth in Levine's assertion that Shakespeare is often perceived to be 'an elite, classic dramatist, to whose plays the bulk of the populace do not or cannot relate'.[20]

Which brings me back to work, a category to which we certainly *can* relate, even as we go about our lives over 400 years after Shakespeare lived his. Might a focus on work in Shakespeare, as this book has sought to provide, help break down some of the potential barriers to reading and appreciating his plays today? Let's think, for instance, about the contemporary experiences of many general readers and audiences, as well as students in secondary schools and universities in England and the United States. Many non-specialist readers and students, especially those encountering Shakespeare's plays for the first time, are likely to think that reading Shakespeare is hard work, at least some of the time. Certainly in my own classrooms, especially at the beginning of the term, students frequently describe reading Shakespeare as challenging, as something that doesn't come naturally to them, as something that may even intimidate them. Reading Shakespeare takes effort: it's not necessarily an easy process, and it's not likely considered 'leisure' reading for most people. But we should also keep in mind that, as we saw in the Introduction, work is a social concept, defined by context rather than by absolutes. Gardening might obviously count as work for someone employed as a professional landscaper, but what about the person who gardens on the weekend at their home? We might ask a similar question about engaging with Shakespeare's plays today. If I attend a performance of *Hamlet* in my spare time, is that leisure? Or is it work, since my job is a professor of Shakespeare studies? Can it be both? What about students attending a school performance of *Hamlet* during a class trip? If something (such as a performance or a reading assignment) is required, does that automatically make it work? And if our modern educational system tends to tip the balance in favour of Shakespeare as work rather than as leisure or play, might there be ways to shift that balance?

As we've seen throughout this book, although many of us may feel today that reading Shakespeare can be hard work, that work isn't one sided. As discussed in Chapter 2, *writing* Shakespeare was also hard work, even though we so often focus on Shakespeare's genius or inspiration rather than the labour (and communal efforts) that went into writing his plays. We often, in other words, have a tendency to follow earlier commentators, such as John Dryden, in viewing Shakespeare himself as an effortless writer, one who created his characters and stories 'not laboriously, but luckily'.[21] But what do we miss if we focus only on Shakespeare as an effortless rather than a 'laborious' or hard-working writer who produced his plays through his attention to craft, deep knowledge of the theatre, and extensive reading? Might a greater appreciation for the *work* that went into Shakespeare's plays bring our experiences closer to those of working-class readers, such as Arch, in the nineteenth century, who considered Shakespeare to be a model for self-improvement achieved through labour? I'd argue that Shakespeare the hard-working writer is a more accessible figure to contemporary readers than Shakespeare the effortless genius. Shakespeare was an artist continually striving to improve his craft, just as many of us aim to do in our own work and lives. Acknowledging Shakespeare's own work as a dramatist thus helps situate him within an everyday, workaday world to which many of us can relate. In turn, this realization can help us read and engage with his plays today with greater enjoyment and understanding.

Not only was Shakespeare a working artist but, as this book has demonstrated, he also wrote about work extensively in his plays. We see this not just in characters who work, such as Bottom and the other mechanicals in *A Midsummer Night's Dream* or servants such as Maria in *Twelfth Night*, or in staged action, such as the reapers who appear in the masque in *The Tempest*, but in the many images of work that pervade his drama and shape it in vital ways. Indeed, once we start looking for work in Shakespeare, it's hard to stop seeing it, even in surprising places like the stylized aristocratic dialogue of *Love's Labour's Lost*, Aaron's scheming in *Titus Andronicus*, or the chants of the witches in *Macbeth*. Realizing just how much Shakespeare engaged with the everyday world of work—something that is central to nearly all of our lives—can, as this book has sought to demonstrate, open up new pathways of understanding for modern readers and audiences, whether they are approaching Shakespeare for the first time or as part of a lifetime of study. Although we can't transport ourselves back to Elizabethan England to capture the immediacy of Shakespeare's language and cultural references, we can tune into his 'working words' and trace a throughline of everyday practices that run through his plays, making way for new insights and points of connection in the process. Such an approach can help us continue to challenge the notion that Shakespeare is an exclusively 'elite' or 'difficult' playwright, in part by encouraging practices of reading that take the everyday—including the labours that make up our daily lives—as seriously as the extraordinary. Taking delight in Shakespeare's language as it engages and is transformed by the quotidian world of work in all its forms is, to my mind, work well done indeed.

Shakespeare and Work. Michelle M. Dowd, Oxford University Press. © Michelle M. Dowd 2026.
DOI: 10.1093/9780191998096.003.0008

Endnotes

INTRODUCTION

1. See Keith Grint and Darren Nixon, *The Sociology of Work*, 4th edn (Cambridge: Polity Press, 2015), Richard H. Hall, *Sociology of Work: Perspectives, Analyses, and Issues* (Thousand Oaks, CA: Pine Forge Press, 1994), and *The Oxford Book of Work*, ed. Keith Thomas (Oxford: Oxford University Press, 1999).
2. *Oxford English Dictionary* I.1.a and II.17.b for 'work', *n.*
3. Tom Rutter, *Work and Play on the Shakespearean Stage* (Cambridge: Cambridge University Press, 2008), 4.
4. Catharina Lis and Hugo Soly, 'Work and Society', in *A Cultural History of Work in the Early Modern Age*, ed. Bert De Munck and Thomas Max Safley (London: Bloomsbury, 2019), 129–44, esp. 129.
5. Rutter, *Work and Play*, 16.
6. See Charles W. Camp, *The Artisan in Elizabethan Literature* (New York: Columbia University Press, 1924), and M. C. Bradbrook, *Shakespeare the Craftsman* (New York: Barnes and Noble, 1969).
7. On the different forms of materialist criticism in relation to Shakespeare studies, see Douglas Bruster, 'The New Materialism in Renaissance Studies', in *Material Cultures and Cultural Materialisms in the Middle Ages and Renaissance*, ed. Curtis Perry (Turnhout: Brepols, 2001), 225–38, and Jean E. Howard, 'Material Shakespeare/Materialist Shakespeare', in *Shakespeare Matters: History, Teaching, Performance*, ed. Lloyd Davis (Newark, DE: University of Delaware Press, 2003), 29–45.
8. Gabriel Egan, *Shakespeare and Marx* (Oxford: Oxford University Press, 2004), 1. See also Jonathan Gil Harris, *Shakespeare and Literary Theory* (Oxford: Oxford University Press, 2010), especially chs 9 and 10.
9. Russ McDonald, *Shakespeare and the Arts of Language* (Oxford: Oxford University Press, 2001), 6.
10. This integration of materialist and aesthetic criticism is sometimes referred to as the 'new' or 'historical formalism' in literary studies. See e.g. *Shakespeare and Historical Formalism*, ed. Stephen Cohen (Aldershot: Ashgate, 2007).
11. For *Measure for Measure*'s connections to early modern city comedy, see Jean E. Howard, 'Shakespeare and Genre', in *A Companion to Shakespeare*, ed. David Scott Kastan (Malden, MA: Blackwell, 1999), 297–310.

12. Alan C. Dessen, *Elizabeth Stage Conventions and Modern Interpreters* (Cambridge: Cambridge University Press, 1984), 34, 12.
13. Caroline F. E. Spurgeon, *Shakespeare's Imagery and What It Tells Us* (New York: Macmillan, 1935), 126.
14. Alison A. Chapman, 'Whose Saint Crispin's Day Is It?', *Renaissance Quarterly* 54 (2001): 1467–94, esp. 1485.
15. See Chapman, 'Whose Saint Crispin's Day Is It', 1487.
16. Northrop Frye, *A Natural Perspective: The Development of Shakespearean Comedy and Romance* (New York: Columbia University Press, 1965), 142.

CHAPTER 1

1. As noted in the Introduction, this book does not aim to be exhaustive in its coverage of different types of work in Shakespeare's plays. One category of work, for instance, that this book does not address in detail is the emerging category of the 'professions' (e.g. lawyers, physicians, and royal administrators). For more on the professions as they relate to Shakespeare's theatre, see Edward Gieskes, *Representing the Professions: Administration, Law, and Theater in Early Modern England* (Newark: University of Delaware Press, 2006).
2. Bert De Munck and Thomas Max Safley, 'Introduction', in *A Cultural History of Work in the Early Modern Age*, ed. Bert De Munck and Thomas Max Safley (London: Bloomsbury, 2019), 1–15, esp. 3.
3. See Crystal Bartolovich, 'Marx's Shakespeare', in *Marx and Freud: Great Shakespeareans*, vol. 10, by Crystal Bartolovich, David Hillman, and Jean E. Howard (London: Bloomsbury, 2012), 7–61.
4. Richard Halpern, *The Poetics of Primitive Accumulation: English Renaissance Culture and the Genealogy of Capital* (Ithaca, NY: Cornell University Press, 1991), 63.
5. Karl Marx, *Capital*, vol. 1, trans. Ben Fowkes (New York: Vintage, 1977), 876.
6. Quoted in *Medieval Political Theory—A Reader: The Quest for the Body Politic, 1100–1400*, ed. Cary J. Nederman and Kate Langdon Forhan (London: Routledge, 1993), 224.
7. Tom Rutter, *Work and Play on the Shakespearean Stage* (Cambridge: Cambridge University Press, 2008), 15.
8. Rutter, *Work and Play*, 15.
9. See Jacques Le Goff, *Medieval Civilization, 400–1500*, trans. Julia Barrow (Oxford: Basil Blackwell, 1988), 261.
10. See Keith Wrighton, *English Society, 1580–1680* (New Brunswick, NJ: Rutgers University Press, 1982), 122, and Steve Rappaport, *Worlds Within*

Worlds: Structures of Life in Sixteenth-Century London (Cambridge: Cambridge University Press, 1989), 64.

11. See Wrighton, *English Society*, 125.
12. See Alexandra Shepard, *Accounting for Oneself: Worth Status, and the Social Order in Early Modern England* (Oxford: Oxford University Press, 2015), 155.
13. Keith Wrightson, *Earthly Necessities: Economic Lives in Early Modern Britain* (New Haven: Yale University Press, 2000), 316.
14. Rutter, *Work and Play*, 19.
15. See Natasha Korda, *Labors Lost: Women's Work and the Early Modern English Stage* (Philadelphia: University of Pennsylvania Press, 2011), 50.
16. See Catharina Lis and Hugo Soly, 'Work and Society', in *A Cultural History of Work in the Early Modern Age*, ed. Bert De Munck and Thomas Max Safley (London: Bloomsbury, 2019), 129–44, esp. 134.
17. 'An Homily Against Idleness', in *The Book of Homilies: A Critical Edition*, ed. Gerald Bray (Cambridge: James Clark & Co., 2015), 483–89, esp. 483.
18. See Mark Netzloff, 'Work', in *The Ashgate Research Companion to Popular Culture in Early Modern England*, ed. Andrew Hadfield, Matthew Dimmock, and Abigail Shinn (Farnham: Ashgate, 2014), 163–76, esp. 169.
19. Quoted in Peter Laslett, *The World We Have Lost* (New York: Charles Scribner's Sons, 1965), 31–2.
20. Ilana Krausman Ben-Amos, *Adolescence and Youth in Early Modern England* (New Haven: Yale University Press, 1994), 42.
21. See Ben-Amos, *Adolescence and Youth*, 39–68.
22. Shepard, *Accounting for Oneself*, 242.
23. The word 'tinker' was itself often associated with itinerancy. The *Oxford English Dictionary* defines a tinker as 'A person who makes a living by mending pots and other metal household utensils, esp. on an itinerant basis' (I.1.a).
24. Shepard, *Accounting for Oneself*, 232.
25. Shepard, *Accounting for Oneself*, 262.
26. See K. Tawny Paul, 'Accounting for Men's Work', *History Workshop Journal* 85 (2018): 26–46. Although Paul's primary focus is on men, he argues that we should be alert to the 'fictions of the archive' that can 'make male work seem so very different from female work' when it was, in many cases, very similar (43).
27. William Ingram, 'The Economics of Playing', in *A Companion to Shakespeare*, ed. David Scott Kastan (Malden, MA: Blackwell, 1999), 318–27, esp. 318.
28. See Rutter, *Work and Play*, 29–33.
29. Walter Cohen, *Drama of a Nation: Public Theater in Renaissance England and Spain* (Ithaca, NY: Cornell University Press, 1985), 181.

30. See M. C. Bradbrook, *Shakespeare the Craftsman* (New York: Barnes and Noble, 1969), 13, and Korda, *Labors Lost*, 24–5.
31. Ingram, 'The Economics of Playing', 320.
32. Gieskes, *Representing the Professions*, 165.
33. See Korda, *Labors Lost*, 25–53.
34. David Kathman, 'Grocers, Goldsmiths, and Drapers: Freemen and Apprentices in the Elizabethan Theater', *Shakespeare Quarterly* 55.1 (2004): 1–49, esp. 3, 2.
35. Roslyn Lander Knutson, *Playing Companies and Commerce in Shakespeare's Time* (Cambridge: Cambridge University Press, 2001), 26, 47.
36. Rutter, *Work and Play*, 48–9.
37. John Northbrooke, *A Treatise Against Dicing, Dancing, Plays, and Interludes, with Other Idle Pastimes* (1577), in *Shakespeare's Theater: A Sourcebook*, ed. Tanya Pollard (Malden, MA: Blackwell, 2004), 1–18, esp. 10.
38. William Rankins, *A Mirror of Monsters* (1587), in *Shakespeare's Theater: A Sourcebook*, ed. Tanya Pollard (Malden, MA: Blackwell, 2004), 124–34, esp. 128.
39. Philip Stubbes, *Anatomy of Abuses* (1583), in *Shakespeare's Theater: A Sourcebook*, ed. Tanya Pollard (Malden, MA: Blackwell, 2004), 115–23, esp. 117, 122.
40. Stephen Gosson, *Plays Confuted in Five Actions* (1582), in *Shakespeare's Theater: A Sourcebook*, ed. Tanya Pollard (Malden, MA: Blackwell, 2004), 84–114, esp. 110.
41. Stephen Gosson, *The School of Abuse* (1579), in *Shakespeare's Theater: A Sourcebook*, ed. Tanya Pollard (Malden, MA: Blackwell, 2004), 19–33, esp. 28.
42. Rutter, *Work and Play*, 36.

CHAPTER 2

1. John. H. Astington, *Actors and Acting in Shakespeare's Time: The Art of Stage Playing* (Cambridge: Cambridge University Press, 2010), 214.
2. See Paul Menzer, *William Shakespeare: A Brief Life* (Bloomsbury: Arden, 2023), 48–9. On the formation of the Queen's Men and their status as a touring company, see also Scott McMillin and Sally-Beth MacLean, *The Queen's Men and Their Plays* (Cambridge: Cambridge University Press, 1998).
3. See Astington, *Actors and Acting*, 214. On Shakespeare's transition from actor to playwright, see Menzer, *William Shakespeare*, 71.
4. Astington, *Actors and Acting*, 214. See also Lucy Munro, *Shakespeare in the Theatre: The King's Men* (London: Bloomsbury, 2020), 5.
5. Janet Dillon, *The Cambridge Introduction to Early English Theatre* (Cambridge: Cambridge University Press, 2006), 111.

6. See Menzer, *William Shakespeare*, 141, 157, and Russ McDonald, *The Bedford Companion to Shakespeare: An Introduction with Documents*, 2nd edn (Boston: Bedford/St Martin's, 2001), 19.
7. Dillon, *Cambridge Introduction*, 76.
8. Roslyn L. Knutson, 'Shakespeare's Repertory', in *A Companion to Shakespeare*, ed. David Scott Kastan (Malden, MA: Blackwell, 1999), 346–61, esp. 351.
9. Roslyn L. Knutson, *Playing Companies and Commerce in Shakespeare's Time* (Cambridge: Cambridge University Press, 2001), 49.
10. Simon Palfrey and Tiffany Stern, *Shakespeare in Parts* (Oxford: Oxford University Press, 2007), 93.
11. Palfrey and Stern, *Shakespeare in Parts*, 4.
12. Menzer, *William Shakespeare*, 107. See also Munro, *Shakespeare in the Theatre*, xvii.
13. Munro, *Shakespeare in the Theatre*, 29.
14. Munro, *Shakespeare in the Theatre*, 29.
15. Tiffany Stern, *Making Shakespeare: From Stage to Page* (London: Routledge, 2004), 67. See also Stern, *Rehearsal from Shakespeare to Sheridan* (Oxford: Oxford University Press, 2000), 71.
16. Stern, *Rehearsal from Shakespeare to Sheridan*, 15.
17. See Stern, *Rehearsal from Shakespeare to Sheridan*, 100–1.
18. *Oxford English Dictionary* 1.a for 'wright', *n.*
19. Scott Newstok, *How to Think Like Shakespeare: Lessons from a Renaissance Education* (Princeton: Princeton University Press, 2020), 137.
20. Emma Smith, 'Shakespeare as Adaptor', in *The Arden Research Handbook of Shakespeare and Adaptation*, ed. Diana E. Henderson and Stephen O'Neill (Bloomsbury: Arden, 2022), 25–37, esp. 25.
21. See Newstok, *How to Think Like Shakespeare*, 38.
22. M. C. Bradbrook, *Shakespeare the Craftsman* (New York: Barnes and Noble, 1969), 75. See also Newstok, *How to Think Like Shakespeare*, 34.
23. Bradbrook, *Shakespeare the Craftsman*, 75.
24. Robert S. Miola, *Shakespeare's Reading* (Oxford: Oxford University Press, 2000), 2.
25. See Miola, *Shakespeare's Reading*, 1–17. In tables 1 and 2, Miola includes very helpful lists of principal source texts and traditions that influenced Shakespeare's works (16). See also Menzer, *William Shakespeare*, 27–8.
26. Astington, *Actors and Acting*, 40.
27. Lynn Enterline, *Shakespeare's Schoolroom: Rhetoric, Discipline, Emotion* (Philadelphia: University of Pennsylvania Press, 2012), 44.
28. Newstok, *How to Think Like Shakespeare*, 80 (italics in original). See also Enterline, *Shakespeare's Schoolroom*, 2–3.

29. Janet Clare, *Shakespeare's Stage Traffic: Imitation, Borrowing and Competition in Renaissance Theatre* (Cambridge: Cambridge University Press, 2014), 4. See also Enterline, *Shakespeare's Schoolroom*, 4, John Kerrigan, *Shakespeare's Originality* (Oxford: Oxford University Press, 2018), 6–7, and Newstok, *How to Think Like Shakespeare*, 74–5.
30. Ben Jonson, *Discoveries*, ed. Lorna Hutson, in *The Cambridge Edition of the Works of Ben Jonson Online*, ed. David Bevington, Marin Butler, and Ian Donaldson (Cambridge: Cambridge University Press, 2014), line 1759.
31. Smith, 'Shakespeare as Adaptor', 25-26. See also Clare, *Shakespeare's Stage Traffic*, 264–5.
32. See Stern, *Making Shakespeare*, 45.
33. Gary Taylor, 'Collaboration 2016', in *Shakespeare in Our Time*, ed. Dympna Callaghan and Suzanne Gossett (Bloomsbury: Arden, 2016), 141–9, esp. 145.
34. Miola, *Shakespeare's Reading*, 154.
35. See Kerrigan, *Shakespeare's Originality*, 15. On commonplace books, see Stern, *Making Shakespeare*, 42.
36. Laurie E. Maguire, 'The Craft of Printing (1600)', in *A Companion to Shakespeare*, ed. David Scott Kastan (Malden, MA: Blackwell, 1999), 434–49, esp. 439.
37. See Stern, *Making Shakespeare*, 153.
38. For more details about the work of the early modern print shop, see Miola, *Shakespeare's Reading*, 10, and Maguire, 'The Craft of Printing (1600)'.
39. See Claire M. L. Bourne, *Typographies of Performance in Early Modern England* (Oxford: Oxford University Press, 2020), 16, and Stern, *Making Shakespeare*, 137–58.
40. John Heminge and Henry Condell, 'To the Great Variety of Readers', in *The Norton Facsimile: The First Folio of Shakespeare*, ed. Charlton Hinman with an introduction by Peter W. M. Blayney, 2nd edn (New York: W. W. Norton, 1996), 7. I have modernized the spelling for ease of reading. It should be noted that Heminge and Condell's authorship of this preface has been questioned since at least the eighteenth century.
41. Jonathan Bate, *Shakespeare and the English Romantic Imagination* (Cambridge: Cambridge University Press, 1986), 6.
42. John Milton, 'On Shakespeare' (lines 9–10), in *The Complete Works of John Milton*, vol. 3, *The Shorter Poems*, ed. Barbara Kiefer Lewalksi and Estelle Haan (Oxford: Oxford University Press, 2012), 25.
43. John Dryden, *An Essay of Dramatick Poesie* (1668) in *The Works of John Dryden*, vol. 17, *Prose 1668–1691: An Essay of Dramatick Poesie and Shorter*

Works, ed. Samual Holt Monk and A. E. Wallace Maurer (Berkeley: University of California Press, 1971), 55.

44. Michael D. Bristol, 'Vernacular Criticism and the Scenes Shakespeare Never Wrote', *Shakespeare Survey* 53 (2000): 89–102, esp. 91, 92.
45. Samuel Johnson, *Preface* (1765) in *The Yale Edition of the Works of Samuel Johnson*, vol. 7, *Johnson on Shakespeare*, ed. Arthur Sherbo (New Haven: Yale University Press, 1968), 59–113, esp. 62, 63.
46. Johnson, *Preface*, 83.
47. Johnson, *Preface*, 72.
48. Johnson, *Preface*, 69.
49. Johnson, *Preface*, 84.
50. Ben Jonson, 'To the Memory of My Beloved, The Author, Master William Shakespeare, And What He Hath Left Us', in *The Cambridge Edition of the Works of Ben Jonson Online*, ed. David Bevington, Martin Butler, and Ian Donaldson (Cambridge: Cambridge University Press, 2014).
51. Laurie Ellinghausen, *Labor and Writing in Early Modern England, 1567–1667* (Burlington, VT: Ashgate, 2008), 13. On Jonson and labour, see also Bruce Boehrer, 'The Poet of Labor: Authorship and Property in the Work of Ben Jonson', *Philological Quarterly* 72.3 (1993): 289–312.
52. For this reference, see Joanna Picciotto, *Labors of Innocence in Early Modern England* (Cambridge, MA: Harvard University Press, 2010), 14.

CHAPTER 3

1. See David Evett, *Discourses of Service in Shakespeare's England* (New York: Palgrave, 2005), 20.
2. David Schalkwyk, *Shakespeare, Love and Service* (Cambridge: Cambridge University Press, 2008), 20. On the difficulties of defining service in the early modern period, see also Mark Thornton Burnett, *Masters and Servants in English Renaissance Drama and Culture* (Basingstoke: Macmillan, 1997), 2–5, and Elizabeth Rivlin, 'Service and Servants in Early Modern English Culture to 1660', *Journal of Early Modern Studies* 4 (2015): 17–41, esp. 18–20.
3. Schalkwyk, *Shakespeare, Love and Service*, 21–4.
4. Interestingly, despite the ubiquity of the concept of hierarchical service in the period, most of the references to 'service' and 'servants' in Shakespeare's plays refer to forms of work rather than broader social or ideological relationships. See Judith Weil, *Service and Dependency in Shakespeare's Plays* (Cambridge: Cambridge University Press, 2005), 2.
5. See Keith Wrightson, *Earthly Necessities: Economic Lives in Early Modern Britain* (New Haven: Yale University Press, 2000), 32–3.

6. A. L. Beier, *Masterless Men: The Vagrancy Problem in England, 1560–1640* (London: Methuen, 1985), 23.
7. Michael Neill, *Putting History to the Question: Power, Politics, and Society in English Renaissance Drama* (New York: Columbia University Press, 2000), 46.
8. Schalkwyk, *Shakespeare, Love and Service*, 9, and Neill, *Putting History to the Question*, 19.
9. See Neill, *Putting History to the Question*, 46.
10. On the large number of servants in Petruchio's country home, see Weil, *Service and Dependency*, 55. On Katherine's 'taming' in terms of household management, see Natasha Korda, *Shakespeare's Domestic Economies: Gender and Property in Early Modern England* (Philadelphia: University of Pennsylvania Press, 2002), 52–75.
11. See Evett, *Discourses of Service*, 56, and Burnett, *Masters and Servants*, 79–80.
12. Schalkwyk, *Shakespeare, Love and Service*, 222.
13. Richard Strier, 'Faithful Servants: Shakespeare's Praise of Disobedience', in *The Historical Renaissance: New Essays on Tudor and Stuart Literature and Culture*, ed. Heather Dubrow and Richard Strier (Chicago: University of Chicago Press, 1988), 104–33, esp. 119.
14. Neill, *Putting History to the Question*, 27.
15. Neill, *Putting History to the Question*, 28.
16. Neill, *Putting History to the Question*, 31.
17. See Sara Mendelson and Patricia Crawford, *Women in Early Modern England* (Oxford: Clarendon Press, 1998), 94.
18. See Eleanor Hubbard, *City Women: Money, Sex, and the Social Order in Early Modern London* (Oxford: Oxford University Press, 2012), 40.
19. On the transition from service to marriage, see Ilana Krausman Ben-Amos, *Adolescence and Youth in Early Modern England* (New Haven: Yale University Press, 1994), 226–32.
20. See Mendelson and Crawford, *Women in Early Modern England*, 102–6.
21. For an extended analysis of women's service in *Twelfth Night*, see Michelle M. Dowd, *Women's Work in Early Modern English Literature and Culture* (New York: Palgrave, 2009), 21–46.
22. Portia in *The Merchant of Venice* is another example of a female protagonist who is notable for her economic skill and household management. See Natasha Korda, *Labors Lost: Women's Work and the Early Modern English Stage* (Philadelphia: University of Pennsylvania Press, 2011), 54–92.
23. Urvashi Chakravarty, *Fictions of Consent: Slavery, Servitude, and Free Service in Early Modern England* (Philadelphia: University of Pennsylvania Press, 2022).

24. Virginia Mason Vaughan and Alden T. Vaughan, '*The Tempest* and Early Modern Conceptions of Race', in *The Cambridge Companion to Shakespeare and Race*, ed. Ayanna Thompson (Cambridge: Cambridge University Press, 2021), 139–57, esp. 145.
25. See Rivlin, 'Service and Servants', 31, and Imtiaz Habib, *Black Lives in the English Archives 1500–1677* (Aldershot: Ashgate, 2008).
26. Vaughan and Vaughan, '*The Tempest*', 146.
27. Patricia Akhimie, *Shakespeare and the Cultivation of Difference: Race and Conduct in the Early Modern World* (New York: Routledge, 2018), 85.
28. Akhimie, *Shakespeare and the Cultivation of Difference*, 93.
29. Akhimie, *Shakespeare and the Cultivation of Difference*, 97.
30. Vaughan and Vaughan, '*The Tempest*', 139.
31. On Prospero's relationship with Ariel, see Chakravarty, *Fictions of Consent*, 178–87, and Vaughan and Vaughan, '*The Tempest*', 144–5.
32. See Vaughan and Vaughan, '*The Tempest*', 142–3.
33. See Vaughan and Vaughan, '*The Tempest*', 140, 144, and 148–50.
34. Vaughan and Vaughan, '*The Tempest*', 153.
35. Akhimie, *Shakespeare and the Cultivation of Difference*, 169–76.
36. See Akhimie, *Shakespeare and the Cultivation of Difference*, 161–3.
37. Akhimie, *Shakespeare and the Cultivation of Difference*, 181.

CHAPTER 4

1. See Ilana Krausman Ben-Amos, *Adolescence and Youth in Early Modern England* (New Haven: Yale University Press, 1994), 88.
2. See Ben-Amos, *Adolescence and Youth*, 84–94, 114–17, Steve Rappaport, *Worlds Within Worlds: Structures of Life in Sixteenth-Century London* (Cambridge: Cambridge University Press, 1989), 291–304, and Keith Wrightson, *Earthly Necessities: Economic Lives in Early Modern Britain* (New Haven: Yale University Press, 2000), 32–3.
3. On women and apprenticeship, see Ben-Amos, *Adolescence and Youth*, and Laura Gowing, *Ingenious Trade: Women and Work in Seventeenth-Century London* (Cambridge: Cambridge University Press, 2022), 55–98.
4. Ben-Amos, *Adolescence and Youth*, 84.
5. Rappaport, *Worlds Within Worlds*, 294.
6. On apprentices, journeymen, and the importance of citizenship, see Rappaport, *Worlds Within Worlds*, 23–9, 184, and 326–7.
7. On theatrical apprenticeships, see John H. Astington, *Actors and Acting in Shakespeare's Time: The Art of Stage Playing* (Cambridge: Cambridge University Press, 2010), 76–107.

8. For Shakespeare as an 'artisan-playwright', see Theodore Leinwand, '"I believe we must leave the killing out": Deference and Accommodation in *A Midsummer Night's Dream*', *Renaissance Papers* (1986): 11–30, esp. 11.
9. On craft workers as audience members, see Charles Whitney, *Early Responses to Renaissance Drama* (Cambridge: Cambridge University Press, 2006), esp. 161–200.
10. On these riots, see e.g. Jennifer C. Vaught, *Carnival and Literature in Early Modern England* (Farnham: Ashgate, 2012), 14.
11. As early as the nineteenth century and the writings of Samual Taylor Coleridge, critics argued that Shakespeare was largely hostile towards common people, including workers. For an early twentieth-century example of this viewpoint, see Charles W. Camp, *The Artisan in Elizabethan Literature* (New York: Columbia University Press, 1924). More recent scholarship, however, has significantly challenged this view, demonstrating instead that Shakespeare takes a much more nuanced and even at times sympathetic approach to artisans and other commoners. For good overviews of this shift in perspective, see Annabel Patterson, *Shakespeare and the Popular Voice* (Cambridge, MA: Blackwell, 1989), and Jeffrey S. Doty, 'Shakespeare and Popular Politics', *Literature Compass* 10.2 (2013): 162–74.
12. See Patricia Parker, *Shakespeare from the Margins: Language, Culture, Context* (Chicago University of Chicago Press), 85.
13. Mark Thornton Burnett, 'Apprentice Literature and the "Crisis" of the 1590s', *The Yearbook of English Studies* 21 (1991): 27–38, esp. 35.
14. On apprentice riots in the 1590s, see Roger B. Manning, *Village Revolts* (Oxford: Oxford University Press, 1988), 187–219, and Rappaport, *World Within Worlds*, 42–60. For the connection between these revolts and *A Midsummer Night's Dream*, see Leinwand, '"I believe we must leave the killing out"', and Patterson, *Shakespeare and the Popular Voice*, 52–70.
15. Leinwand, '"I believe we must leave the killing out"', 19. See also Ronda Arab, *Manly Mechanicals on the Early Modern English Stage* (Selinsgrove, PA: Susquehanna University Press, 2011), 115–17.
16. For the favourable representation of Bottom's masculinity in the play, see Arab, *Manly Mechanicals*, 112–15.
17. Tom Rutter, *Work and Play on the Shakespearean Stage* (Cambridge: Cambridge University Press, 2008), 50.
18. Rutter, *Work and Play*, 50.
19. See Andy Wood, *Riot, Rebellion and Popular Politics in Early Modern England* (Basingstoke: Palgrave, 2002), 40–2.
20. Doty, 'Shakespeare and Popular Politics', 163.

21. As John Michael Archer notes, the 'law' that Flavius invokes here (that the workers should be bearing the 'sign' of their profession) is simple 'stage law', since 'neither Romans nor Londoners bore mandated "signs" of their trades'. See *Citizen Shakespeare: Freemen and Aliens in the Language of the Plays* (New York: Palgrave, 2005), 132.
22. Archer, *Citizen Shakespeare*, 132.
23. As Archer writes of the Roman tragedies, 'contemporary London, with its livery company vocabulary and economic conception of citizenship as the practice of a trade, keeps piercing the surface of Shakespeare's depiction of Rome'. See *Citizen Shakespeare*, 123.
24. See Patterson, *Shakespeare and the Popular Voice*, 137.
25. See Archer, *Citizen Shakespeare*, 142.
26. See Patterson, *Shakespeare and the Popular Voice*, 38–9.
27. On the scenes between Peter and Horner, see Archer, *Citizen Shakespeare*, 74–6, and Mark Thornton Burnett, *Masters and Servants in English Renaissance Drama and Culture: Authority and Obedience* (Basingstoke: Macmillan, 1997), 20–1.
28. See Arab, *Manly Mechanicals*, 107.
29. See Arab, *Manly Mechanicals*, 76–7. On the connection between the artisans' occupations and their imagined violence, see also Archer, *Citizen Shakespeare*, 79.
30. On the positive aspects of Shakespeare's representation of Cade, see Arab, *Manly Mechanicals*, 70–93, Chris Fitter, *Radical Shakespeare: Politics and Stagecraft in the Early Career* (London: Routledge, 2012), Patterson, *Shakespeare and the Popular Voice*, 32–51, and Andy Wood, 'Brave Minds and Hard Hands: Work, Drama, and Social Relations in the Hungry 1590s', in *Shakespeare and the Politics of Commoners: Digesting the New Social History*, ed. Chris Fitter (Oxford: Oxford University Press, 2017), 84–101.
31. See Vaught, *Carnival and Literature*, 14.
32. See Manning, *Village Revolts*, 197, and Frederick Tupper, Jr., 'The Shakespearean Mob', *PMLA* 27.4 (1912): 486–523, esp. 491. See also the *Oxford English Dictionary* definition I.1.d for 'clubs', which connects the word to the phrase 'prentices and clubs: the rallying cry of the London apprentices' and cites Hall.
33. See e.g. T. F. Thiselton Dyer's discussion of 'clubs' in *Folklore of Shakespeare* (New York, 1883). Dyer, citing Edmond Malone, notes that 'it was once a common custom, on the breaking out of a fray, to call out "Clubs, clubs!" to part the combatants', but he goes on to note: '"Clubs," too, was originally the popular cry to call forth the London apprentices, who employed

their clubs for the preservation of the public peace. Sometimes, however, they used those weapons to raise a disturbance' (492).

34. A cry which may or may not be heard by the brothers. Modern editors give the cry of 'clubs, clubs', to Aaron as an aside, although there is no dramaturgical reason for excluding Chiron and Demetrius from hearing this line. Regardless, Aaron's exclamation would certainly have resonated with the audience and, as such, it helps to fuel a series of important cultural associations between violence, apprentice labour, and national or social identity.
35. Ian Archer, *The Pursuit of Stability: Social Relations in Elizabethan London* (Cambridge: Cambridge University Press, 1991), 17.

CHAPTER 5

1. *The Agrarian History of England and Wales*, vol. 4, *1500–1640*, ed. Joan Thirsk (Cambridge: Cambridge University Press, 1967), 398.
2. See *The Agrarian History of England and Wales*, 4.417–18, and Ilana Krausman Ben-Amos, *Adolescence and Youth in Early Modern England* (New Haven: Yale University Press, 1994), 73–83.
3. On the seasonal nature of agricultural work, see *The Agrarian History of England and Wales*, 4.166–7, and François Laroque, *Shakespeare's Festive World: Elizabethan Seasonal Entertainment and the Professional Stage*, trans. Janet Lloyd (Cambridge: Cambridge University Press, 1991), 90–2.
4. Joanna Picciotto, *Labors of Innocence in Early Modern England* (Cambridge, MA: Harvard University Press, 2010), 45. See also Bridget Ann Henisch, *The Medieval Calendar Year* (University Park: Pennsylvania State University Press, 1999).
5. See Charlotte Scott, *Shakespeare's Nature: From Cultivation to Culture* (Oxford: Oxford University Press, 2014), 16.
6. Thomas Tusser, *Five Hundred Points of Good Husbandry* (Oxford: Oxford University Press, 1984 [London, 1580]), 41.
7. Andrew McRae, *God Speed the Plough: The Representation of Agrarian England, 1500–1660* (Cambridge: Cambridge University Press, 1996), 13.
8. See McRae, *God Speed the Plough*, 12–17, Mark Netzloff, 'Work', in *The Ashgate Research Companion to Popular Culture in Early Modern England*, ed. Andrew Hadfield, Matthew Dimmock, and Abigail Shinn (Farnham: Ashgate, 2014), 163–76, esp. 171–2, Keith Wrightson, *Earthly Necessities: Economic Lives in Early Modern Britain* (New Haven: Yale University Press, 2000), 160–4, and *The Agrarian History of England and Wales.*
9. Scott, *Shakespeare's Nature*, 16–17.

10. See Craig Muldrew, 'The "Middling Sort": An Emergent Cultural Identity', in *A Social History of England, 1500–1750*, ed. Keith Wrightson (Cambridge: Cambridge University Press, 2017), 290–309, esp. 299–300, and *The Agrarian History of England and Wales*, 4.161–3.
11. See *The Agrarian History of England and Wales*, 4.200–12, Netzloff, 'Work', 171–2, and Wrightson, *Earthly Necessities*, 102–4.
12. McRae, *God Speed the Plough*, 16, and Muldrew, 'The "Middling Sort"', 299.
13. On enclosure as it relates to Cade's rebellion in *2 Henry VI*, see Ronda Arab, *Manly Mechanicals on the Early Modern English Stage* (Selinsgrove, PA: Susquehanna University Press, 2011), 78–82, and McRae, *God Speed the Plough*, 117–18.
14. Northrop Frye, *A Natural Perspective: The Development of Shakespearean Comedy and Romance* (New York: Columbia University Press, 1965), 142.
15. Northrop Frye, *Anatomy of Criticism: Four Essays* (Princeton: Princeton University Press, 1957), 183.
16. Frye, *Anatomy of Criticism*, 183. See also Frye, *A Natural Perspective*, 141. On the ritual, festive structure of Shakespearian comedy, see also C. L. Barber, *Shakespeare's Festive Comedy: A Study in Dramatic Form and Its Relation to Social Custom* (Princeton: Princeton University Press, 1959).
17. Raymond Williams, *The Country and the City* (Oxford: Oxford University Press, 1973), 32.
18. Adam Zucker, *The Places of Wit in Early Modern English Comedy* (Cambridge: Cambridge University Press, 2011), 145.
19. On the relationship between pastoral and agrarian work, see Katherine C. Little, *Transforming Work: Early Modern Pastoral and Late Medieval Poetry* (Notre Dame, IN: University of Notre Dame Press, 2013), 8–9.
20. See Scott, *Shakespeare's Nature*, 22.
21. On Shakespeare's indebtedness to the festival calendar, see Laroque, *Shakespeare's Festive World*.
22. See Scott, *Shakespeare's Nature*, 4.
23. For instance, in the early twentieth century, Caroline Spurgeon argued that Shakespeare's references to farming are 'very small in number'. See *Shakespeare's Imagery and What It Tells Us* (Cambridge: Cambridge University Press, 1935), 46.
24. Scott, *Shakespeare's Nature*, 27.
25. Robert F. G. Spier and Donald K. Anderson, Jr., 'Shakespeare and Farming: The Bard and Tusser', *Agricultural History* 59.3 (1985): 448–61, esp. 452.

26. On the connections between *As You Like It* and the enclosure movement, see Richard Wilson, '"Like the Old Robin Hood": *As You Like It* and the Enclosure Riots', *Shakespeare Quarterly* 43.1 (1992): 1–19.
27. For the connection between the harvest, seasonality, and the masque in *The Tempest*, see Laroque, *Shakespeare's Festive World*, 221–2, and Scott, *Shakespeare's Nature*, chapter 6.
28. See Ronald Hutton, *The Stations of the Sun: A History of the Ritual Year in Britain* (Oxford: Oxford University Press, 1996), 322, Laroque, *Shakespeare's Festive World*, 217–21, and Scott, *Shakespeare's Nature*, ch. 5.
29. On Act 4 as a pastoral transition from the first part of the play to its conclusion, see Laroque, *Shakespeare's Festive World*, 217–21.
30. Louis A. Montrose, '*Love's Labour's Lost* and the Politics of Play', *Texas Studies in Literature and Language* 18.4 (1977): 528–52, esp. 529, 547.
31. On the play's rhetorical and linguistic devices, see William C. Carroll, *The Great Feast of Language in 'Love's Labour's Lost'* (Princeton: Princeton University Press, 1976), and Keir Elam, *Shakespeare's Universe of Discourse: Language Games in the Comedies* (New York: Cambridge University Press, 1984), 289–308.
32. On this line in the context of early modern farming, see Spier and Anderson, 'Shakespeare and Farming', 453.
33. See *Love's Labour's Lost*, The Arden Shakespeare, 3rd series, ed. H. R. Woodhuysen (London: Bloomsbury, 1998), 118 n. 97. For a description of the breeding period of geese as in the spring, see also Charles Stevens and John Liebault, *Maison Rustique, or The Countrie Farme*, trans. Richard Surflet (London, 1600), 106.
34. The King's focus on precise markers of time at the outset of the play also signals a tension between the artificial and the natural, with the former ultimately giving way to the latter. On this point see Catherine M. McLay, 'The Dialogues of Spring and Winter: A Key to the Unity of Love's Labour's Lost', *Shakespeare Quarterly* 18.2 (1967): 119–27, esp. 122.
35. Armado similarly links farming with fertility vis-à-vis romantic love in his bawdy claim that he has 'vowed to Jaquenetta | To hold the plough for her sweet love three years' (5.2.869–70).
36. See Dympna Callaghan, 'Confounded by Winter: Speeding Time in Shakespeare's Sonnets', in *A Companion to Shakespeare's Sonnets*, ed. Michael Schoenfeldt (Malden, MA: Blackwell, 2007), 104–17, esp. 109.
37. Montrose, '*Love's Labour's Lost* and the Politics of Play', 538. See also Barber, who writes: 'each song says, in a marvelously economical way, where people are in the cycle of the year, the people of farm, manor or village who live entirely in the turning seasons' (*Shakespeare's Festive Comedy*, 133).

38. On human cultivation as a means of imposing order on nature, see Scott, *Shakespeare's Nature*.

CHAPTER 6

1. Craig Muldrew, *The Economy of Obligation: The Culture of Credit and Social Relations in Early Modern England* (Basingstoke: Macmillan, 1998), 19.
2. Robert Brenner, *Merchants and Revolution: Commercial Change, Politic Conflict and London's Overseas Traders, 1550–1653* (Cambridge: Cambridge University Press, 1993), 43. See also Muldrew, *Economy of Obligation*, 20.
3. See Keith Wrightson, *English Society 1580–1680* (New Brunswick, NJ: Rutgers University Press, 1995), 27–8.
4. See Theodore Leinwand, *Theatre, Finance, and Society in Early Modern England* (Cambridge: Cambridge University Press, 1999), 129.
5. L. C. Knights, *Drama and Society in the Age of Jonson* (London: Chatto and Windus, 1937), 51–2.
6. Mark Netzloff, *England's Internal Colonies: Class, Capital, and the Literature of Early Modern Colonialism* (New York: Palgrave, 2004), 33.
7. Merry Wiesner-Hanks, 'Do Women Need the Renaissance?', *Gender and History* 20.3 (2008): 539–57, esp. 550. On England's growing colonial econ omy, see also Leinwand, *Theatre, Finance, and Society*, 119, and Muldrew, *Economy of Obligation*, 54–5.
8. Andrew McRae, *God Speed the Plough: The Representation of Agrarian England, 1500–1660* (Cambridge: Cambridge University Press, 1996), 168. See also Netzloff, *England's Internal Colonies*, 12–13.
9. Muldrew, *The Economy of Obligation*, 96–7.
10. McRae, *God Speed the Plough*, 168. See also Katherine C. Little, *Transforming Work: Early Modern Pastoral and Late Medieval Poetry* (Notre Dame, IN: University of Notre Dame Press, 2013), 93–4.
11. Tom Rutter, *Work and Play on the Shakespearean Stage* (Cambridge: Cambridge University Press, 2008), 16.
12. Rutter, *Work and Play*, 16.
13. See David Hawkes, *The Culture of Usury in Renaissance England* (New York: Palgrave, 2010), 121.
14. See Valerie Forman, *Tragicomic Redemptions: Global Economics and the Early Modern England Stage* (Philadelphia: University of Pennsylvania Press, 2008), 22–3.
15. See *The Agrarian History of England and Wales*, vol. 4 *1500–1640*, ed. Joan Thirsk (Cambridge: Cambridge University Press, 1967), 568–9.
16. Rutter, *Work and Play*, 132.
17. See Netzloff, *England's Internal Colonies*, 20–35.

18. See Jean E. Howard, 'Shakespeare and Genre', in *A Companion to Shakespeare*, ed. David Scott Kastan (Malden, MA: Blackwell, 1999), 297–310.
19. Charlotte Scott, *Shakespeare's Nature: From Cultivation to Culture* (Oxford: Oxford University Press, 2014), 163.
20. Scott, *Shakespeare's Nature*, 189.
21. Scott, *Shakespeare's Nature*, 190.
22. François Laroque, *Shakespeare's Festive World: Elizabethan Seasonal Entertainment and the Professional Stage*, trans. Janet Lloyd (Cambridge: Cambridge University Press, 1991), 222.
23. Scott, *Shakespeare's Nature*, 188.
24. See Scott, *Shakespeare's Nature*, 213–14.
25. Scott, *Shakespeare's Nature*, 14.
26. Virginia Mason Vaughan and Alden T. Vaughan, '*The Tempest* and Early Modern Conceptions of Race', in *The Cambridge Companion to Shakespeare and Race*, ed. Ayanna Thompson (Cambridge: Cambridge University Press, 2021), 139–57, esp. 139. For how the play 'advocates a model of colonial labor', see also Netzloff, *England's Internal Colonies*, 131.
27. Patricia Akhimie, *Shakespeare and the Cultivation of Difference: Race and Conduct in the Early Modern World* (New York: Routledge, 2018), 159.
28. Akhimie notes that in the masque, 'Prospero builds on the illusion of a labor-free farm'. *Shakespeare and the Cultivation of Difference*, 160.
29. Daniel Vitkus, 'Labor and Travel on the Early Modern Stage: Representing the Travail of Travel in Dekker's *Old Fortunatus* and Shakespeare's *Pericles*', in *Working Subjects in Early Modern English Drama*, ed. Michelle M. Dowd and Natasha Korda (Farnham: Ashgate Publishing, 2011), 225–42, esp. 234.
30. See *The Cambridge World History of Food*, ed. Kenneth F. Kiple and Kriemhild Coneè Ornelas (Cambridge: Cambridge University Press, 2015), 359–64, and *The Oxford Companion to Food*, 3rd edn, ed. Alan Davidson (Oxford: Oxford University Press, 2014), 169–70.
31. See *Cambridge World History of Food*, 361, and Paolo Squatriti, *Landscape and Change in Early Medieval Italy: Chestnuts, Economy, and Culture* (Cambridge: Cambridge University Press, 2013), 48–9.
32. *Cambridge World History of Food*, 362.
33. See Squatriti, *Landscape and Change*, 39–41, and *Cambridge World History of Food*, 362.
34. See Laroque, *Shakespeare's Festive World*, 82.
35. Laroque, *Shakespeare's Festive World*, 157–8, 159.
36. Laroque, *Shakespeare's Festive World*, 158.
37. On Falstaff as a carnivalesque character or 'Lord of Misrule', see C. L. Barber, *Shakespeare's Festive Comedy: A Study in Dramatic Form and Its Relation to Social Custom* (Princeton: Princeton University Press, 1959).

EPILOGUE

1. Quoted in Andrew Murphy, *Shakespeare for the People: Working-Class Readers, 1800–1900* (Cambridge: Cambridge University Press, 2008), 156.
2. See Murphy, *Shakespeare for the People*, esp. 155–7.
3. John Dryden, *An Essay of Dramatick Poesie* (1668) in *The Works of John Dryden*, vol. 17, *Prose 1668–1691: An Essay of Dramatick Poesie and Shorter Works*, ed. Samual Holt Monk and A. E. Wallace Maurer (Berkeley: University of California Press, 1971), 55.
4. See Douglas Lanier, *Shakespeare and Modern Popular Culture* (Oxford: Oxford University Press, 2002), 26–33.
5. Lanier, *Shakespeare and Modern Popular Culture*, 33.
6. Murphy, *Shakespeare for the People*, 39, 48–50.
7. Murphy, *Shakespeare for the People*, 69.
8. Murphy, *Shakespeare for the People*, 75.
9. See Lanier, *Shakespeare and Modern Popular Culture*, 36–7, and Lawrence W. Levine, *Highbrow/Lowbrow: The Emergence of Cultural Hierarchy in America* (Cambridge, MA: Harvard University Press, 1988).
10. Jonathan Bate, *Shakespearean Constitutions: Politics, Theatre, Criticism, 1730–1830* (Oxford: Clarendon Press, 1989), 64.
11. See Antony Taylor, 'Shakespeare and Radicalism: The Uses and Abuses of Shakespeare in Nineteenth-Century Popular Politics', *The Historical Journal* 45.2 (2002): 357–79, esp. 357 and 369.
12. See Levine, *Highbrow/Lowbrow*, 63–5, and Lanier, *Shakespeare and Modern Popular Culture*, 39.
13. Quoted in Levine, *Highbrow/Lowbrow*, 65.
14. Murphy, *Shakespeare for the People*, 138.
15. Murphy, *Shakespeare for the People*, 173. For an overview of changes in working-class engagement with Shakespeare during this period, see Murphy, *Shakespeare for the People*, 162–97.
16. Lanier, *Shakespeare and Modern Popular Culture*, 42.
17. Levine, *Highbrow/Lowbrow*, 68, 76. See also Murphy, *Shakespeare for the People*, 174–5.
18. Levine, *Highbrow/Lowbrow*, 77. See also Lanier, *Shakespeare and Modern Popular Culture*, 39–42.
19. Denise Albanese, *Extramural Shakespeare* (New York: Palgrave, 2010), 5.
20. Levine, *Highbrow/Lowbrow*, 34.
21. Dryden, *An Essay of Dramatick Poesie*, 55.

Further Reading

Shakespeare's World of Work

Work, as we discussed in the Introduction, can be a difficult subject to pin down. A good place to start is Keith Grint and Darren Nixon, *The Sociology of Work*, 4th edn (Cambridge: Polity Press, 2015), which provides a comprehensive introduction to sociological approaches to work as a category, encompassing topics such as gender, the global economy, and work and identity. In a similar vein, Richard H. Hall, *Sociology of Work: Perspectives, Analyses, and Issues* (Thousand Oaks, CA: Pine Forge Press, 1994) offers students an introductory textbook that covers a wide range of topics related to the sociology of work, including social mobility, unemployment, and contingent labour. For a book-length overview that is more grounded in the literary-historical world, *The Oxford Book of Work*, ed. Keith Thomas (Oxford: Oxford University Press, 1999) opens with a highly readable and informative introductory essay, while the text itself consists of over 500 excerpts about work by famous writers, including Charles Dickens, Mark Twain, and Dorothy Parker.

For readers interested in the history of work in early modern England, there are several studies that will provide excellent guidance. Peter Laslett's classic study *The World We Have Lost* (New York: Charles Scribner's Sons, 1965) helped to reshape the historical understanding of early modern England by focusing on everyday life, and it remains an engaging read and a good starting point for further study. For more recent examinations of social and economic conditions in England, Keith Wrightson's *English Society, 1580–1680* (New Brunswick, NJ: Rutgers University Press, 1982) and *Earthly Necessities: Economic Lives in Early Modern Britain* (New Haven: Yale University Press, 2000) offer readers clear and detailed analysis of the socio-economic changes that marked the sixteenth and seventeenth centuries. Focusing on London as an urban centre, Steve Rappaport in *Worlds Within Worlds: Structures of Life in Sixteenth-Century London* (Cambridge: Cambridge University Press, 1989) takes a more conservative approach to these changes, emphasizing the stability and resilience of London society. In *Accounting for Oneself: Worth, Status, and the Social Order in Early Modern England* (Oxford: Oxford University Press, 2015), Alexandra Shepard investigates how early modern people understood their place in the social hierarchy, providing cogent discussion of such topics as credit, ways of making a living, and the gendered division of labour. For broader historical overviews of early modern work, readers can consult

A Cultural History of Work in the Early Modern Age, ed. Bert De Munck and Thomas Max Safley (London: Bloomsbury, 2019) and Mark Netzloff's chapter on 'Work', in *The Ashgate Research Companion to Popular Culture in Early Modern England*, ed. Andrew Hadfield, Matthew Dimmock, and Abigail Shinn, 163–76 (Farnham: Ashgate, 2014).

For those interested in how work and working people were represented in the drama of Shakespeare and his contemporaries, two older studies are worthy of attention. While Charles W. Camp's *The Artisan in Elizabethan Literature* (New York: Columbia University Press, 1924) takes a largely negative view of Shakespeare's depiction of labourers, in *Shakespeare's Imagery and What It Tells Us* (New York: Macmillan, 1935), Caroline F. E. Spurgeon draws attention to the ways in which Shakespeare's language often refers to early modern trades and crafts. In a more recent study, Tom Rutter's *Work and Play on the Shakespearean Stage* (Cambridge: Cambridge University Press, 2008) offers the most comprehensive approach to the topic, with a focus on how the early modern theatre's own problematic relationship to work influenced how it dramatized labour. *Working Subjects in Early Modern English Drama*, ed. Michelle M. Dowd and Natasha Korda (Farnham: Ashgate Publishing, 2011) provides a series of essays on work and identity that considers a wide range of dramatic texts. In *Shakespeare's Labored Art: Stir, Work, and the Late Plays* (New York: Peter Lang, 1995), Maurice Hunt discusses labour as a theme in Shakespeare's romances. Edward Gieskes explores dramatic portrayals of the emerging professions in *Representing the Professions: Administration, Law, and Theater in Early Modern England* (Newark: University of Delaware Press, 2006). For the connection between the London livery companies and the professional theatre, see David Kathman, 'Grocers, Goldsmiths, and Drapers: Freemen and Apprentices in the Elizabethan Theater', *Shakespeare Quarterly* 55.1 (2004): 1–49. Natasha Korda's *Labors Lost: Women's Work and the Early Modern English Stage* (Philadelphia: University of Pennsylvania Press, 2011) is an excellent resource for those interested in how women's labour shaped the early modern stage. On women's work, see also Fiona McNeill, *Poor Women in Shakespeare* (Cambridge: Cambridge University Press, 2007) and Michelle M. Dowd, *Women's Work in Early Modern English Literature and Culture* (New York: Palgrave, 2009), which examines women's writing in addition to dramatic sources.

Shakespeare as Working Artist

Shakespeare's career as an artist was multifaceted, encompassing his work both as an actor and as a playwright. For those interested in the general habits of mind and approaches to craft that may have shaped Shakespeare's writing, an excellent place to start is Scott Newstok's highly engaging *How to Think Like Shakespeare: Lessons from a Renaissance Education* (Princeton: Princeton University Press, 2020). Tiffany Stern's *Making Shakespeare: From Stage to Page* (London: Routledge, 2004) is another useful and readable introduction that emphasizes how Shakespeare's plays were formed through his engagement with both theatrical and print culture. In *Shakespeare the Craftsman* (New York: Barnes and Noble, 1969), M. C. Bradbrook offers a more traditional assessment of Shakespeare's status as a craftsman and how he responded to changing theatrical demands. There are an abundance of sources covering the professional theatre in Shakespeare's time, but readers specifically interested in the labour, craft, and economic practices of the theatre can turn to several important studies. Two excellent books that consider the economic context of the early professional theatres are William Ingram, *The Business of Playing: The Beginnings of the Adult Professional Theater in Elizabethan London* (Ithaca, NY: Cornell University Press, 1992) and Roslyn L. Knutson, *Playing Companies and Commerce in Shakespeare's Time* (Cambridge: Cambridge University Press, 2001). For the work of acting in particular, including Shakespeare's own career as an actor, see John. H. Astington, *Actors and Acting in Shakespeare's Time: The Art of Stage Playing* (Cambridge: Cambridge University Press, 2010). On the specific technology of the part-script and how it impacted the work of acting and playwrighting, see Simon Palfrey and Tiffany Stern, *Shakespeare in Parts* (Oxford: Oxford University Press, 2007). On the labour of rehearsal, see Tiffany Stern, *Rehearsal from Shakespeare to Sheridan* (Oxford: Oxford University Press, 2000).

Shakespeare's labour as a playwright included his education, his reading habits, and his processes of revision. An excellent starting point is Robert S. Miola, *Shakespeare's Reading* (Oxford: Oxford University Press, 2000), part of the same series as the current volume. On Shakespeare's education and how it influenced his plays, readers should consult Lynn Enterline, *Shakespeare's Schoolroom: Rhetoric, Discipline, Emotion* (Philadelphia: University of Pennsylvania Press, 2012). For discussion of Shakespeare's practice of borrowing material from other authors, a central component of humanist practices in the period, see Janet Clare, *Shakespeare's Stage Traffic: Imitation, Borrowing and Competition in Renaissance Theatre* (Cambridge: Cambridge University Press, 2014) and John Kerrigan, *Shakespeare's Originality* (Oxford: Oxford University Press, 2018). For those interested more broadly in the concept of vocation as it pertained specifically to writing in the period, Laurie Ellinghausen, *Labor and Writing in Early Modern England, 1567–1667* (Burlington, VT: Ashgate, 2008) provides a useful account that focuses on a range of non-aristocratic authors.

Service and Domestic Work

Domestic labour in Shakespeare's England has been the subject of numerous studies in recent years, with service receiving particular attention. For how the Shakespearian stage depicted domestic work and the gendered division of labour, both Wendy Wall's *Staging Domesticity: Household Work and English Identity in Early Modern Drama* (Cambridge: Cambridge University Press, 2002) and Natasha Korda's *Shakespeare's Domestic Economies: Gender and Property in Early Modern England* (Philadelphia: University of Pennsylvania Press, 2002) are essential reads. Two useful historical accounts that give attention to the early modern service economy (and also discuss artisans and apprentices, a topic covered below) are A. L. Beier, *Masterless Men: The Vagrancy Problem in England, 1560–1640* (London: Methuen, 1985) and Ilana Krausman Ben-Amos, *Adolescence and Youth in Early Modern England* (New Haven: Yale University Press, 1994). Elizabeth Rivlin's review essay 'Service and Servants in Early Modern English Culture to 1660', *Journal of Early Modern Studies* 4 (2015): 17–41, offers readers an excellent introduction to the subject that includes both historical and literary perspectives.

Several volumes consider servants and service in early modern drama. Mark Thornton Burnett's important study *Masters and Servants in English Renaissance Drama and Culture* (Basingstoke: Macmillan, 1997) examines master–servant relationships in a range of plays, focusing on questions of power and social change. Several chapters of Michael Neill's *Putting History to the Question: Power, Politics, and Society in English Renaissance Drama* (New York: Columbia University Press, 2000) turn their attention to service, in works by both Shakespeare and his contemporaries. A more exclusive focus on Shakespeare's plays can be found in David Evett, *Discourses of Service in Shakespeare's England* (New York: Palgrave, 2005), Judith Weil, *Service and Dependency in Shakespeare's Plays* (Cambridge: Cambridge University Press, 2005), and David Schalkwyk, *Shakespeare, Love and Service* (Cambridge: Cambridge University Press, 2008), which also includes discussion of the sonnets. For service as it relates to practices of racialized slavery in Shakespeare's plays and early modern literary texts more broadly, two particularly groundbreaking volumes deserve attention: Patricia Akhimie, *Shakespeare and the Cultivation of Difference: Race and Conduct in the Early Modern World* (New York: Routledge, 2018) and Urvashi Chakravarty, *Fictions of Consent: Slavery, Servitude, and Free Service in Early Modern England* (Philadelphia: University of Pennsylvania Press, 2022).

Artisans and Apprentices

In addition to the general historical studies cited above (especially Beier, Ben-Amos, Wrightson, and Rappaport), readers interested in learning more about

Shakespeare's dramatization of artisans and apprentices can consult a range of sources. Camp's *The Artisan in Elizabethan Literature* (mentioned above) argues for Shakespeare's fundamental hostility to workers. However, more recent studies have challenged this position, offering more nuanced accounts of Shakespeare's depictions of artisanal labour. For good overviews of these critical shifts, see Annabel Patterson, *Shakespeare and the Popular Voice* (Cambridge, MA: Blackwell, 1989) and Jeffrey S. Doty, 'Shakespeare and Popular Politics', *Literature Compass* 10.2 (2013): 162–74.

Two excellent studies that consider how Shakespeare and other early modern dramatists staged artisans and other craft workers are John Michael Archer, *Citizen Shakespeare: Freemen and Aliens in the Language of the Plays* (New York: Palgrave, 2005), which usefully examines Shakespeare's language rather than direct stage representations, and Ronda Arab, *Manly Mechanicals on the Early Modern English Stage* (Selinsgrove, PA: Susquehanna University Press, 2011), which explores staged representations of labouring men and how they helped shape ideas about masculinity. Theodore Leinwand's article '"I believe we must leave the killing out": Deference and Accommodation in *A Midsummer Night's Dream*', *Renaissance Papers* (1986): 11–30, provides not only a compelling argument about this particular comedy, but also a good overview of how representations of artisans touched on social concerns about riot and disorder. For more on the apprentice riots of the 1590s, see Roger B. Manning, *Village Revolts* (Oxford: Oxford University Press, 1988), Mark Thornton Burnett, 'Apprentice Literature and the "Crisis" of the 1590s', *The Yearbook of English Studies* 21 (1991): 27–38, and Andy Wood, *Riot, Rebellion and Popular Politics in Early Modern England* (Basingstoke: Palgrave, 2002). On women as apprentices, see Laura Gowing, *Ingenious Trade: Women and Work in Seventeenth-Century London* (Cambridge: Cambridge University Press, 2022). Those interested in the role of artisans as theatrical audience members should consult Charles Whitney, *Early Responses to Renaissance Drama* (Cambridge: Cambridge University Press, 2006), especially chapter 4.

Working the Green World

Agrarian labour has not received as much attention in Shakespeare as have other forms of work, but several important historical and literary studies consider agricultural production, the rural economy, and ideas about the natural world more generally. The most comprehensive historical resource remains *The Agrarian History of England and Wales*, vol. 4, *1500–1640*, ed. Joan Thirsk (Cambridge: Cambridge University Press, 1967), a monumental study of agrarian practices and important changes in England's rural economy during Shakespeare's lifetime. For those interested in how literary depictions of agrarian labour changed across the late medieval and into the early modern period, Katherine C. Little's *Transforming Work: Early Modern Pastoral and Late Medieval Poetry* (Notre Dame, IN: University of Notre Dame Press, 2013), provides a compelling account. In *Shakespeare's Nature: From Cultivation to Culture* (Oxford: Oxford University Press, 2014), Charlotte Scott explores Shakespeare's engagement with contemporary practices of farming and land management and how these contexts influenced his plays. In their article 'Shakespeare and Farming: The Bard and Tusser', *Agricultural History* 59.3 (1985): 448–61, Robert F. G. Spier and Donald K. Anderson, Jr offer a succinct and highly informative account of Shakespeare's many textual references to farming. In *God Speed the Plough: The Representation of Agrarian England, 1500–1660* (Cambridge: Cambridge University Press, 1996), Andrew McRae takes a more interdisciplinary approach, considering a wide range of historical and literary texts to trace changes in England's rural economy.

Several studies examine Shakespeare's depiction of the natural world, including his representation of rural festivals related to agrarian labour. For a good overview of this subject, see Tom MacFaul, *Shakespeare and the Natural World* (Cambridge: Cambridge University Press, 2015). On the topic of the literary 'green world', which features so prominently in many of Shakespeare's plays, readers should consult two important works by Northrop Frye: *Anatomy of Criticism: Four Essays* (Princeton: Princeton University Press, 1957) and *A Natural Perspective: The Development of Shakespearean Comedy and Romance* (New York: Columbia University Press, 1965). On the relationship between the green world and labour, see Raymond Williams, *The Country and the City* (Oxford: Oxford University Press, 1973). C. L. Barber addresses the festive dimensions of Shakespeare's plays in *Shakespeare's Festive Comedy: A Study in Dramatic Form and Its Relation to Social Custom* (Princeton: Princeton University Press, 1959). On Shakespeare's engagement with the seasonal patterns of the rural economy, see François Laroque, *Shakespeare's Festive World: Elizabethan Seasonal Entertainment and the Professional Stage*, trans. Janet Lloyd (Cambridge: Cambridge University Press, 1991). Those interested in a comprehensive historical account of the many agrarian festivals and other activities that take place across the year in England should consult Ronald Hutton, *The Stations of the Sun: A History of the Ritual Year in Britain* (Oxford: Oxford University Press, 1996).

Going to Market

There has been a great deal of interest in recent years in early modern England's developing capitalist economy and the many forms of labour, including venture capitalism, overseas trade, and novel forms of investment and commercial enterprise, that it supported. On the rise in England's consumer economy, see Joan Thirsk, *Economic Policy and Projects: The Development of a Consumer Society in Early Modern England* (Oxford: Clarendon Press, 1978) and Craig Muldrew, *The Economy of Obligation: The Culture of Credit and Social Relations in Early Modern England* (Basingstoke: Macmillan, 1998). On the growth of England's overseas trade during this period, see Robert Brenner, *Merchants and Revolution: Commercial Change, Politic Conflict and London's Overseas Traders, 1550–1653* (Cambridge: Cambridge University Press, 1993). For a comparativist approach to the development of England's global trade routes in a colonialist context, see Alison Games, *The Web of Empire: English Cosmopolitans in an Age of Expansion, 1560–1660* (Oxford: Oxford University Press, 2008).

On how the early modern theatre depicted these newer forms of commercial labour, L. C. Knights, *Drama and Society in the Age of Jonson* (London: Chatto and Windus, 1937) offers an early account that considers (among other topics) the important role of joint-stock companies. In *Theatre, Finance, and Society in Early Modern England* (Cambridge: Cambridge University Press, 1999), Theodore Leinwand examines such topics as credit, debit, and capital ventures as they pertain to period drama. Valerie Forman focuses on global trade in relation to the genre of tragicomedy in *Tragicomic Redemptions: Global Economics and the Early Modern England Stage* (Philadelphia: University of Pennsylvania Press, 2008). For another approach to England and colonialism that discusses a range of literary materials and emphasizes the connection between domestic and overseas colonies, see Mark Netzloff, *England's Internal Colonies: Class, Capital, and the Literature of Early Modern Colonialism* (New York: Palgrave, 2004). The essays collected in *Money and the Age of Shakespeare: Essays in New Economic Criticism*, ed. Linda Woodbridge (New York: Palgrave, 2003) consider England's commercial economy from a variety of perspectives, with attention to Shakespeare's *Twelfth Night*, *The Merchant of Venice*, *The Winter's Tale*, and *Measure for Measure*, among other works.

Shakespeare and the Working Class

Finally, for those interested in learning more about the complex yet fascinating history of Shakespeare's adoption (and rejection) by working-class readers and audiences since the nineteenth century, an excellent place to start is Andrew Murphy's *Shakespeare for the People: Working-Class Readers, 1800–1900* (Cambridge: Cambridge University Press, 2008). Those wishing to compare the nineteenth-century context with that of the previous century should consult Jonathan Bate, *Shakespearean Constitutions: Politics, Theatre, Criticism, 1730–1830* (Oxford: Clarendon Press, 1989). In *Shakespeare and Modern Popular Culture* (Oxford: Oxford University Press, 2002), another volume in the Oxford

Shakespeare Topics series, Douglas Lanier provides a clear and compelling overview of how Shakespeare's position vis-à-vis popular culture has changed across the twentieth century. In his classic account, *Highbrow/Lowbrow: The Emergence of Cultural Hierarchy in America* (Cambridge, MA: Harvard University Press, 1988), Lawrence W. Levine devotes considerable attention to Shakespeare and his gradual transformation from a favourite of the working classes in nineteenth-century America to a hallmark of elite culture in the twentieth. For a different perspective, one that situates Shakespeare as a central part of public culture in the United States by the beginning of the twenty-first century, see Denise Albanese, *Extramural Shakespeare* (New York: Palgrave, 2010).

General Bibliography

Akhimie, Patricia. *Shakespeare and the Cultivation of Difference: Race and Conduct in the Early Modern World.* New York: Routledge, 2018.

Arab, Ronda. *Manly Mechanicals on the Early Modern English Stage.* Selinsgrove, PA: Susquehanna University Press, 2011.

Archer, John Michael. *Citizen Shakespeare: Freemen and Aliens in the Language of the Plays.* New York: Palgrave, 2005.

Astington, John H. *Actors and Acting in Shakespeare's Time: The Art of Stage Playing.* Cambridge: Cambridge University Press, 2010.

Ben-Amos, Ilana Krausman. *Adolescence and Youth in Early Modern England.* New Haven: Yale University Press, 1994.

Bradbrook, M. C. *Shakespeare the Craftsman.* New York: Barnes and Noble, 1969.

Bruster, Douglas. *Drama and the Market in the Age of Shakespeare.* Cambridge: Cambridge University Press, 1992.

Burnett, Mark Thornton. *Masters and Servants in English Renaissance Drama and Culture.* Basingstoke: Macmillan, 1997.

Camp, Charles W. *The Artisan in Elizabethan Literature.* New York: Columbia University Press, 1924.

Chakravarty, Urvashi. *Fictions of Consent: Slavery, Servitude, and Free Service in Early Modern England.* Philadelphia: University of Pennsylvania Press, 2022.

Clark, Alice. *Working Life of Women in the Seventeenth Century.* London: Routledge, 1919; 3rd edn, 1992.

Dowd, Michelle M. *Women's Work in Early Modern English Literature and Culture.* New York: Palgrave, 2009.

Dowd, Michelle M. and Natasha Korda, eds. *Working Subjects in Early Modern English Drama.* Farnham: Ashgate Publishing, 2011.

Ellinghausen, Laurie. *Labor and Writing in Early Modern England, 1567–1667.* Burlington, VT: Ashgate, 2008.

Gieskes, Edward. *Representing the Professions: Administration, Law, and Theater in Early Modern England.* Newark: University of Delaware Press, 2006.

Gowing, Laura. *Ingenious Trade: Women and Work in Seventeenth-Century London.* Cambridge: Cambridge University Press, 2022.

Ingram, William. *The Business of Playing: The Beginnings of Adult Professional Theater in Elizabethan London.* Ithaca, NY: Cornell University Press, 1992.

Korda, Natasha. *Labors Lost: Women's Work and the Early Modern English Stage*. Philadelphia: University of Pennsylvania Press, 2011.

Laroque, François. *Shakespeare's Festive World: Elizabethan Seasonal Entertainment and the Professional Stage*. Trans. Janet Lloyd. Cambridge: Cambridge University Press, 1991.

Leinwand, Theodore B. *Theatre, Finance, and Society in Early Modern England*. Cambridge: Cambridge University Press, 1999.

McRae, Andrew. *God Speed the Plough: The Representation of Agrarian England, 1500–1660*. Cambridge: Cambridge University Press, 1996.

Murphy, Andrew. *Shakespeare for the People: Working-Class Readers, 1800–1900*. Cambridge: Cambridge University Press, 2008.

Patterson, Annabel. *Shakespeare and the Popular Voice*. Cambridge, MA: Blackwell, 1989.

Rappaport, Steve. *Worlds Within Worlds: Structures of Life in Sixteenth-Century London*. Cambridge: Cambridge University Press, 1989.

Rutter, Tom. *Work and Play on the Shakespearean Stage*. Cambridge: Cambridge University Press, 2008.

Scott, Charlotte. *Shakespeare's Nature: From Cultivation to Culture*. Oxford: Oxford University Press, 2014.

Stevenson, Laura Caroline. *Praise and Paradox: Merchants and Craftsmen in Elizabethan Popular Literature*. Cambridge: Cambridge University Press, 1984.

Thirsk, Joan, ed. *The Agrarian History of England and Wales*. Vol. 4, *1500–1640*. Cambridge: Cambridge University Press, 1967.

Wall, Wendy. *Staging Domesticity: Household Work and English Identity in Early Modern Drama*. Cambridge: Cambridge University Press, 2002.

Wrightson, Keith. *Earthly Necessities: Economic Lives in Early Modern Britain*. New Haven: Yale University Press, 2000.

Index

Note: Figures are indicated by an italic *f*.

For the benefit of digital users, indexed terms that span two pages (e.g., 52–53) may, on occasion, appear on only one of those pages.